Navigating the Legal Minefields of Private Investigations

A Career-Saving Guide for Private Investigators, Detectives, and Security Police

RON HANKIN

43-08 162nd Street
Flushing, NY 11358
www.LooseleafLaw.com
800-647-5547

This publication is not intended to replace nor be a substitute for any official procedural material issued by your agency of employment or other official source. Looseleaf Law Publications, Inc., the author and any associated advisors have made all possible efforts to ensure the accuracy and thoroughness of the information provided herein but accept no liability whatsoever for injury, legal action or other adverse results following the application or adoption of the information contained in this book.

Library of Congress Cataloging-In-Publication Data

Hankin, Ronald M.
 Navigating the legal minefield of private investigations : a career-saving guide for private investigators, detectives & security police / Ronald M. Hankin.
     p. cm.
 Includes index.
 ISBN 978-1-932777-73-4
 1. Police, Private--Legal status, laws, etc.--United States. 2. Private investigators--Legal status, laws, etc.--United States. 3. Private security--Law and legislation--United States. I. Title.
  KF5399.5.P7H35 2009
  344.7305'289--dc22

                                        2008034808

Printed in the United States of America

Cover design by *Sans Serif, Inc.* Saline, Michigan

2nd Printing 2009
3rd Printing 2011
4th Printing 2012

Table of Contents

I

*To Cam, Craig, Makenzie, Kylie,
and in Loving Memory of Kirk, son, brother and uncle*

*— and to our little companions, some here, some gone,
who have brought so much joy to everyone they touched:*

Mindy, Mork, Maggie, Missy, Mandy and Polly

—and to my stalwarts Bill Carlson, USMC and Dick Nelson

Suspecting fraud, the insurers put a *gumshoe* on the case. {The gumshoe} came back with a blunt report. "My feeling about this claim," he told his superiors, "is about the same as someone trying to make me swallow a 3 lb. fish. First of all, I dislike fish, second, I surely wouldn't try to swallow it whole, especially when it offends my sense of smell the way this claim does. *Terra Nova Ins. Co. v. Associates Commercial*, 697 FSupp 1048 (ED Wis 1988). (Emphasis provided)

What, you might ask, is a Gumshoe?

There is argument about the origin of the term *gumshoe*; although there is no argument about to whom it refers: *the private detective.*

Various theories and urban legend contribute to the term's origin: take your pick since all are undocumented:

In days of yore, the boot worn by the private detective was an early version of the gym shoe. Made of gum rubber, the advantage of the gumshoe boot was that it did not squeak as he prowled the streets and alleys, gun drawn, looking for clues.

Later, particularly the 40s and 50s, the private detective was continually out and about, moving in dark shadows, and very apt to get gum or other substances stuck to his fine leather soles.

Today, the private detective is not as concerned about his footwear as he is about sticking to his quarry like, well ...gum.

Times have changed, but not the idea: The *Gumshoe* is still a privately-hired sleuth operating in a hostile world, doing what he has to do to expose thievery, fraud and other misdeeds for the betterment of his client and society in general—while staying within the law.

Ah, the rub—the law!

R on Hankin earned his bachelor's degree from the Medill School of Journalism, Northwestern University, and his Juris Doctor from Chicago's IIT Kent College of Law. He served the U.S. Marine Corps as rifle company commander and Commanding Officer of Security for the Navy prison, San Diego, California, and left the Corps a Major. He then served the FBI under J. Edgar Hoover as Special Agent working criminal investigations and fugitive apprehension, before entering the private practice of law.

During the past twenty years, he has also operated a private detective agency specializing in domestic surveillance. In his free time, he is a commercial pilot. As owner-pilot of over twenty aircraft during his flying career, Ron has participated in air shows throughout the Midwest in his authentically restored Marine Corps SNJ "Texan," Marine Corps SNB "Twin Beech," and Marine Corps AT-19, "Gullwing Reliant" patrol plane.

He lives in a suburb northwest of Chicago with wife Camille and black Labradors, Mandy and Polly.

Foreword

Working the detective and security fields without a lawyer in the next seat is precarious at best. The private operative is awash in law on a daily basis—criminal law, civil law, licensing law, administrative law, and even municipal trash collection law. No single book could ever summarize the myriad of federal and state laws that regulate the private detective and security professions. In fact, a series of books would find difficulty accomplishing such a feat. That in mind, what *Navigating the Legal Minefield of Private Investigations* attempts is to supply enough legal authority and precedent that the operative has some general understanding of the issues governing the case at hand, permitting a head-start on his local research—*ALWAYS* mindful one's own state constitution and statutes may provide constraints exceeding those cases highlighted in the Handbook.

About the Handbook layout:

Part I is directed to private operatives—we know them as licensed private detectives and private security officers. Included are legal topics that most concern the working private detective or security officer.

Part II is directed to private special police. These are licensed operatives who have been granted police-like authority by virtue of some statute or ordinance. The legal topics included are those most commonly encountered by private special police, though by no means unique to private special police: much of the case law governing private special police derive from incidences involving regular police.

There is considerable crossover in the topics, since some topics apply equally to both the private operative and the private special police officer. Thus, a particular topic may be found in one part but applicable to both; for example, the polygraph.

Some chapters open with editorial license: a vignette demonstrating the law at work. These situations are very real and involve instances that at least one working detective has encountered during his career.

In essence, the handbook contains no legal advice, just general study principles; and while it is not to be considered the final word on any particular aspect of the profession, it is designed to be a good place to start one's own personal research.

A final note: As in the opening example, *Sentry Sec., In Re,* 417 A2d 190 (Pa 1980), the tendency of the courts is to use the male pronoun in referring to private detectives and police officers. For purposes of consistency, so will this Handbook, notwithstanding that the author knows the investigative field, both private and public, is replete with female operatives. Of course, no offense is intended to any of my female colleagues.

Part I

The Authority and Liability of Private Operatives

By virtue of this Act, {the private detective} is permitted to intrude upon the privacy of individuals and other entities in multiple areas...In conferring such *awesome power*...the state...has prescribed *strict qualifications* for those who would become licensed detectives. *Sentry Sec., Inc., In re, 417 A2d 190, 195 (Pa 1980).*
(Emphasis provided)

1.1   INTRODUCTION

Private operatives—we know them as private detectives and private security officers—derive their lawful authority from the state in which they are licensed. Some states refer to its private sleuth as "private investigator," but, label notwithstanding, the authority and liabilities remain the same. The typical licensing act limits the issuance of these sought-after licenses to applicants of good moral character with prior government-police or police-like civilian experience. Most state statutes require true detective or supervisory police experience to fill the role of licensed private operative. Patrolmen need not apply.

In Pennsylvania, the qualities that are looked for in a private operative were discussed by that state's Supreme court in *Sentry Sec. Inc.* [1] In *Sentry,* the court revoked the license of an operative who had overstated his qualifications to be a private detective. The Pennsylvania licensing law required that a licensed detective be previously "regularly employed as a detective, or shall have been a member of the United States Government investigative service, a sheriff, or member of a city police department of a rank or grade

3

higher than that of a patrolman for a period of not less than three years {prior to licensing}." But, in fact, the detective in question had been a patrolman for some of the three years. The court discussed the reasoning for the stringent requirement:

The Private Detective Act was designed to afford the citizens the service of detectives whose reputation, moral character and ability were beyond reproach. The emphasis {is} to restrict this privilege to only the best qualified, both morally and by training. Unlike the normal policeman, the private detective does not have the supervision of a hierarchy of the…department in which he serves. He makes the judgments as to the manner in which he acts and the matters in which he becomes involved. By virtue of this Act, he is permitted to intrude upon the privacy of individuals and other entities in multiple areas…In conferring such *awesome power*, the state, through its legislature…has pre-scribed strict qualifications for those who would become licensed detectives (emphasis added). [2]

Private detectives and their security counterparts are authorized to exercise their statutory authority in a variety of tasks, some mundane but complex, others dangerous and even more complex. Often these private operative assign-ments overlap those of law enforcement—in fact, they frequently butt!—since private operatives can also be found investigating crimes as varied as murder, arson and theft—nonetheless, the private operative is more akin to some solitary outpost than part of mainstream law enforcement. The private operative, in particular the private detective, truly serves alone in a hostile environment.

1.2   STATUTORY AUTHORITY OF PRIVATE DETECTIVES

The statutory authority of the private detective is summarized in a sample statute, *The Illinois Private Detective and Private Security Act of 1993, 225 ILCS 446/5*:

Private Detective means any person who ...engages in the business of...

1) Investigation of crime and wrongs done under the laws of the United States or the state of licensing;
2) Investigating the habits, conduct, business occupation, honesty, integrity, credibility, knowledge, trustworthiness, efficiency, loyalty, activity, movements, whereabouts, affiliations, associations, transactions, acts, reputation, or character of any person, firm, association or corporation, by any means, manually or electronically;
3) Recovery of lost or stolen property;
4) Securing evidence to be used in court;
5) Determining the cause and origin of fires;
6) Service of process;
7) Locating of lost and missing persons, and the protection of property.
8) Protection of individuals from bodily harm or death (bodyguard function).

1.3   STATUTORY AUTHORITY OF PRIVATE SECURITY OPERATIVES

The statutory authority of private security is summarized in another sample statute, *The Private Detective and Private Security Act of 1993, 225 ILCS 446/5*:

Private Security Contractor means any person who engages in the business of providing a private guard, watchman, patrol service, or any like service by any other title or name on a contractual basis for another person, firm, association, or corporation for a fee or other valuable consideration and performing one or more of the following functions:

5

1) Prevention or detection of intrusion, entry, theft, van-
   dalism, abuse, fire, or trespass on private or governmental property;
2) Prevention, observation, or detection of any unauthorized activity on private or governmental property;
3) Protection of patrons and persons lawfully authorized
   to be on the premises protected;
4) Prevention of the misappropriation or concealment of
   goods, money, bonds, stocks, notes, valuable documents or papers;
5) Protection of individuals from bodily harm or death
   (bodyguard function).

A quick perusal of both the detective and security statutes assures us the private operative's authority is expansive, pervasive and intrusive. It is paramount to an understanding of the breadth of a gumshoe's authority to reiterate that every accused or civil defendant is entitled to a complete investigation to determine facts that absolve him from wrongdoing or establish his cause. Time after time what stands between a client and jail or a million dollar judgment is the diligence and vigilance of his private detective.

It is clear the gumshoe has statutory authority to investigate any matter, criminal or civil, for which he is hired; and can go wherever in the state the facts take him. This responsibility is a mirror of the responsibility of law enforcement; no less important. Just opposite sides: every accused or defendant has a constitutional right to a proper defense; and any detective must understand that he does not owe an explanation to any police officer before interviewing a witness to his client's cause. In fact, the private detective would be derelict were he to allow a police officer to block him from such an interview; the judge or lawyer handling the case derelict for permitting a police officer to impede the detective in this mission; and the police officer guilty of obstruction of justice for advising a witness not to talk to the private detective. [3]

On the other hand, the private detective is not a law officer and the gumshoe's authority may surprise for what it does not include. In theory, at least, a private operative is a bad guy to have angry at you: he can investigate you, track you down, interrogate you, serve you papers, and even protect others from you, or you from others, but the private operative can not arrest you for a crime he did not witness, but believes you committed, unless he's prepared to be sued if he's wrong.

1.4	**PRIVATE OPERATIVE'S LAWFUL AUTHORITY TO ARREST**

Despite the "awesome" authority referred to by the court in *Sentry* (this chapter, page 3) and delineated in the sample statute (this chapter, page 5), a private operative has less authority to arrest a miscreant than a school teacher who suspects a student slipped a book under his coat (See **School Security**, page 193).

Arrest Authority
"An arrest, as the term is used in the criminal law, signifies the apprehension or detention of the person of another in order that he may be forthcoming to answer for an alleged or supposed crime." [4]

Under the common law and most state statutes the private operative has only the arrest authority of a private person: he may arrest another when he has probable cause to believe the subject is committing an offense (other than a city ordinance violation) *in his presence*. If he arrests for an offense outside his presence, guessing there was a crime or who was the perpetrator, and is wrong, he is liable. [5]

Probable Cause
Simply put, probable cause is the linchpin of criminal law, the backdrop to the law of arrest, search and seizure, and merchant detainment. The existence of probable cause constitutes a defense against any claim of false arrest. What is probable cause? An arresting party acts on probable cause when he arrests on facts which lead "a reasonable person of ordinary caution and prudence to believe, or to entertain an

honest suspicion, that the subject committed the offense {in question}." [6]

Since private operatives include among their ranks investigators working major investigations as varied and important as nuclear and industrial security breaches, arson and homicide investigations, amongst a litany of others, one might be surprised to find the law has not chiseled out an exception authorizing the private operative to arrest on probable cause for offenses committed outside their presence. But neither the common law nor state legislatures have seen fit to authorize this authority—with two exceptions: the retail merchant security officer who is given arrest-like authority to counter shoplifting; and the private special police officer who has quasi-police authority on property owned or protected by his employer.

Retail Merchant Security

Under the common law, a retail merchant was liable if he arrested a shoplifter for a crime he did not witness and the thief had managed to discard the item before apprehension. The merchant was charged with false arrest: he did not have grounds to arrest for an act he did not witness and there was no evidence of crime. [7] Modern retail theft statutes resolve this risk. Under the statutes of many states, merchant security is authorized to make an arrest-like "detainment" of a suspect even when he, the security officer, did not personally witness the theft. These retail merchant theft statutes provide immunity from claims of false arrest for merchant security so long as the detainment is based on probable cause or some equivalent, such as "reasonable grounds to suspect." [8] ("Reasonable grounds," tantamount to probable cause, should not be confused with "reasonable suspicion," a lesser standard espoused in **Terry v. Ohio**. See **Reasonable Suspicion**, Page 181).

In Illinois, a sample statute, *Offense of Retail Theft, 720 ILCS 5/16 A-5,* reads:

Detention: Any merchant who has reasonable grounds to believe that a person has committed retail theft may detain such person, on or off the premises of a retail mercantile establishment, in a reasonable manner and for a reasonable length of time for all or any of the following purposes:

    (a) To request identification;
    (b) To verify such identification;
    (c) To make reasonable inquiry as to whether such person has in his possession unpurchased merchandise and to make reasonable investigation of the ownership of such merchandise;
    (d) To inform a peace officer of the detention of the person and surrender that person to the custody of a peace officer.

5/16A-6: Affirmative defense. A detention as permitted in this Article does not constitute an arrest or an unlawful restraint...nor shall it make the merchant liable to the person so detained.

Private Special Police

A private special police officer is a licensed private detective or security officer with police-like authority. (See **Private Special Police, Basis of Authority**, page 121) The private special police officer has authority which sets him apart from his private operative counterpart. By virtue of state statute, city ordinance, or agreement with authorized governmental agency, private special police have the same or similar authority as that of regular police but limited to the employer's venue.

This delegated broadening of an operative's authority was discussed in 1980 by the *D.C. Court of Appeals* in *United States v. Lima*:

The courts have distinguished actions of private security guards from those of commissioned deputized special police officers for good reasons. Although both are privately employed with a duty to protect property of their employer, the special police officer or deputized officer is commonly vested by the state with powers beyond that of the ordinary citizen... In contrast, a licensed security officer has only the power of arrest of an ordinary citizen. [9]

 Warning Since the arrest and search authority of private special police mirrors regular law enforcement, private special police officers also face the same potential for liability under federal civil rights laws as regular police. (See **Color of Law**, Sect. 1983 Liability, page 122)

1.5	PRIVATE OPERATIVE: FORCE IN MAKING CITIZEN'S ARREST

A private operative has the arrest authority of a private party, and "is normally justified in the use of force which he reasonably believes to be necessary to affect the arrest short of force which can cause death or great bodily harm." For instance, enough physical force may be used by a private operative to "effectively" restrain a thief who would rather run than wait for police. [10]

Retail Merchant Security: Lawful Force in Making a Detainment

A retail merchant security operative has statutory authority to use "reasonable force" to detain a theft suspect. Reasonable force includes authority to pursue him off the property should he flee, and handcuffs as needed to restrain him. [11]

1.6	PRIVATE OPERATIVE: AUTHORITY TO DEFEND PERSONS AND PROPERTY

The brunt of our nation's security work is handled by private operatives: be he bodyguard, store and facility security officer, armored truck and bank guard, or private detective, all function in a hazardous environment, with prospects ripe for injury or death to themselves or a member of the public. The authority to protect people and things is a high-risk endeavor and is regulated by the statutes of the state in which the private operative operates. While there is no universal law amongst the states of an operative's authority to defend himself, others or their property, general rules do emerge.

Defense of Person

In self-defense of himself or another person, a private operative may use reasonable and necessary force to counter unlawful force. However, deadly force may be used only if he reasonably believes such extreme force and nothing less will prevent imminent death or great bodily harm to himself or another. [12]

In some states, retreat would be required in preference to deadly force. However, in the "majority of states, the law imposes no duty to retreat on one who acts in self-defense and who was not the original aggressor." [13] In such states, force may be repelled with force, "even to the extent of taking the attacker's life, if necessary." [14]

> *In Michigan,* the state's Supreme Court stated the general rule:
> {T}he killing of another person in self-defense...by one free of fault is justifiable homicide if, under all the circumstances, he honestly and reasonably believes that he is in imminent danger of death or great bodily harm and that it is necessary to exercise deadly force....{He} is never required to retreat from a sudden, fierce, and violent attack; nor is he required to retreat from an attacker who he reasonably believes is about to use a deadly weapon. [15]

Defense of Dwelling (his own)

The operative, like any citizen, may protect his dwelling against another's entry or damage to the extent he reasonably believes that such action is necessary to terminate the entry or attack. Deadly force may be used only when the entry is made in violent manner and the operative reasonably believes such force is needed to prevent an assault on someone in the dwelling, or to prevent a felony in the dwelling. [16] In some jurisdictions, not all, he is not required to retreat before using deadly force. [17]

Defense of Property (including a dwelling not his own)

More pertinent to the private operative's usual duties in the protection of property is his authority to use reasonable force to terminate a trespass on or other criminal interference with property—real and personal— in his charge. However, he is justified in the use of deadly force or force likely to cause great bodily harm only if he reasonably believes such force is necessary to prevent the commission of a forcible felony. [18]

What is a forcible felony? A lot of dastardly things; but a quick review shows that not every felony which occasionally results in violence makes the list; whereas, those which involve force or threat of force at the onset do. [19]

Here are those which Florida and Illinois list:

Florida: "...treason; murder; manslaughter; sexual battery; carjacking; home-invasion robbery; robbery; burglary; arson; kidnapping; aggravated assault; aggravated battery; aggravated stalking; aircraft piracy; unlawful throwing, placing, or discharging of a destructive device or bomb; and any other felony which involves the use or threat of physical force or violence against any individual. *§776.08, FL Stat. (2000)*

Illinois: "...first degree murder, second degree murder, predatory criminal sexual assault of a child, aggravated criminal sexual assault, criminal sexual assault, robbery, burglary, residential burglary, aggravated arson, arson...." *720 ILCS 5/2-8 (1998).*

1.7   PRIVATE OPERATIVE'S RIGHT TO SEARCH

The Fourth Amendment ensures the right of all persons to be secure in their person, houses, papers, and effects against "unreasonable searches and seizures." The language thereby includes arrests—seizure of the person—and searches of his things—houses, papers, and effects. To begin any discussion of the private operative's right to search we refer to the Fourth Amendment for guidance. The Amendment is specifically directed at government action only, not actions of the private operative. It is established law that unless there is shown some connection ("nexus") between the private operative and the government, sufficient to make the private operative an agent of the government, the Fourth Amendment is irrelevant to the action of a private detective or security personnel. [20] (See **Color of Law**, page 122).

The fact a private operative's actions lie outside the Fourth Amendment is not lost on prosecutors who use the materials in prosecution regardless of how the operative came upon them. This accepted principle stems from the 1921 U.S. Supreme Court decision of *Burdeau v. McDowell.*

> In *Burdeau*, the Court held that notwithstanding criminal tactics of private detectives in "retrieving" materials from Burdeau, the evidence could be used in court against him because the illegal retrieval was outside the parameters of the Fourth Amendment. None of this means, however, that a private operative is exempt from prosecution for theft or other illegal actions in conducting a search. [21] (See **Liability of Private Operatives**, page 17)

Retail Merchant Search

Many states authorize the retail merchant and his security to "…make reasonable inquiry as to whether such person has in his possession unpurchased merchandise." (From a sample statute, *Illinois: Offense of Retail Theft, 720 ILCS 5/16 A-6 (c)(1998)*) Some jurisdictions define "reasonable inquiry" to mean a "search to recover stolen merchandise." [22] Also, there is authority that a merchant may protect himself with a pat-down to guard against hidden weapons. [23]

Warning
Local laws must be gauged before emptying someone's pockets looking for stolen merchandise or weapons: *In Ohio,* any search in conjunction with a merchant detention is illegal. Unless the merchant security has private special police authority, the merchant may hold the suspect for police but may not search him. [24]

Chapter 1 - Table of Authorities

1.   *Sentry Sec. Inc., In re,* 417 A2d 190, 195-196 (Pa 1980).

2.   *Sentry Sec. Inc., In re,* 417 A2d 190, 195-196 (Pa 1980).

3.   *Stevens v. Delaware Correctional Center,* 152 FSupp2d 561, 568 (D.Del 2001).

4.   *State v. Champion,* 622 P2d 905, 910 (Wash 1981).

5.   *Gontarez et al v. Smitty's Super Valu, Inc.,* 680 P2d 807, 812 (Ariz 1984).

6.   *Burghardt v. Remiyac,* 565 NE2d 1049, 1052 (Ill 1991).

7.   *Gontarez et al v. Smitty's Super Valu, Inc.,* 680 P2d 807, 812 (Ariz 1984).

8.   *Com. v. McElroy,* 630 A2d 35, 38 (Pa 1993): "Difference is semantics." *Parker v. State,* 502 A2d 510, 516 (Md. 1985): "Tantamount." *Gontarez et al v. Smitty's Super Valu, Inc.,* 680 P2d 807, 813 (Ariz 1984). "Same meaning."

9.   *United States v. Lima,* 424 A2d 113, 119 (DC 1980).

10. *People v. Harmon,* 558 NE2d 173, 175 (Ill 1990).

11. *Peters v. Menards,* 589 NW2d 395, 402 (Wis 1999).

12. *People v. Riddle,* 2002 MI 1899 (MI 2002).

13. *State v. Williams,* 916 P2d 445, 450 (Wash 1996).

14. *People v. Bush,* 111 NE2d 326, 328 (Ill 1953).

15. *People v. Riddle,* 2002 Mi 1899 (Mi 2002).

16. *People v. Morris,* 516 NE2d 412, 418 (Ill 1987).

17. *State v. Carothers,* 594 NW2d 897, 900 (Minn 1999).

18. *People v. Raber,* 264 NE2d 274, 275 (Ill 1970).

19. *State v. Hearns,* 961 So2d 211, 215 (Fla 2007).

20. *Burdeau v. McDowell,* 256 U.S. 465 (1921).

21. *Burdeau v. McDowell,* 256 U.S. 465 (1921).

22. *White v. State,* 572 P2d 569 (Okl 1977).

23. *Collom v. State,* 673 P2d 904 (Al 1983).

24. *Davis v. May Department Stores,* 2001 OH 4537, (55) (Oh 2001).

The nexus required for {employer's liability}...is the incident leading to injury must be an "outgrowth" of the employment; the risk of tortuous injury must be "inherent in the working environment" or "typical of...the {employer's} enterprise." *Lisa M. Henry Mayo*, 48 CalRptr2d 510, 514 (Cal 1995).

2.1   INTRODUCTION

T he duties of a private detective or security officer, take your pick, are fraught with confrontation; it can be a violent and deadly occupation for the operative as well as the general public. Liability for injury to third persons hangs over any private operative and his employer. However, exposed as he is to tort liability for injury to the public, he has nowhere near the exposure of his brethren with quasi-police powers—private special police officers—who face an even darker cloud of liability—the potential of near unlimited liability for acts a citizen alleges deprived him of his federal civil rights. (See **Liability: State Tort and Section 1983**, page 122)

Doubtless, then, there is ample liability to go around, not just for the operative himself, but also for his employer. The law shows little compassion for the employer who was not present when the injurious act occurred. Simply put, an employer's liability is vicarious, attaching as though he were present and authorized the employee to fire a bullet at a suspected miscreant when he had no basis in law to do so. Liability to the absentee boss commonly attaches in one of two ways:

- through the doctrine of *respondeat superior* ("let the master answer") or
- by employer negligence in hiring, training, or supervising the security officer who pulled the trigger. [1]

2.2	**RESPONDEAT SUPERIOR**

Under the doctrine of respondeat superior, an employer is liable for acts of an employee in the scope of the employee's duties. The principle applies to acts that "as a practical matter are sure to occur in the conduct of the employer's business." [2]

In Illinois, the state Supreme Court decided a 1977 case involving an on-duty doctor who drugged a patient on hospital premises in order to sexually assault her. The Court said the act was not work related and explained its application of respondeat superior:

If an employee commits an intentional tort with the dual purpose of furthering the employer's interest and venting personal anger, respondeat superior will lie; however, if the employee acts purely in his own interest, liability under respondeat superior is inappropriate...Thus, an employer was not liable for the criminal act of its employee-watchman in setting fire to the building which he had been employed to guard, or for the shooting of a trespasser who was leaving the employer's premises by a guard who was armed without the knowledge or permission of the employer, or where the employee engaged in a fistfight for purposes unrelated to his job, or where the employee-driver deviated from the route leading to the destination assigned by the employer. On the other hand, the employer was held liable where an employee-brakeman who had been instructed to remove unauthorized riders on railroad cars willfully and maliciously pulled a boy off a moving train, crushing the latter's foot in the process, and where the employee mistakenly injured the plaintiff in defending the employer's property against robbers. [3]

There is divergence amongst states whether respondeat superior includes actions of off-duty police used as part-time security when faced with criminality on the protected property after the conclusion of their shift. In some jurisdictions, police officers are directed to take action when faced with crime regardless of whether they are "on the clock." Since they may face department discipline if they do not act, their off-duty actions are usually not attributed to the private employer, but rather to governmental entity which employs them on a full-time basis. [4]

2.3   EMPLOYER'S NEGLIGENCE

The employer may also find himself liable for acts of an incompetent employee, separate and apart from respondeat superior. This extension of liability is based on a simple premise: the employer did the hiring and knew, or should have known, the employee was dumb, untrained, ill-equipped for the task at hand, or all of the above. [5] It takes little imagination to envision the havoc which might occur when an untrained employee is used in security work.

In a 1996 *D.C. Court of Appeals* decision, facts showed that a supervisor authorized an untrained janitor to stand-in for a security guard who did not show for work. To help him do his job, the supervisor issued the janitor a loaded weapon with hair trigger. A few hours later an innocent visitor who took a wrong turn in the building lay bleeding from a gunshot wound. The security company was, of course, held liable. [6]

2.4   EMPLOYEE-EMPLOYER LIABILITY

Volumes crowd the shelf reciting the criminal and civil wrongs committed by employees that resulted in catastrophic liability for themselves and their employers. To the variety of innocent misdeeds add the litany of injuries arising from the confrontational nature of the private operative's occupation.

False Arrest-False Imprisonment

The charges share the same elements: the subject was held against his will when there was no probable cause to arrest him. The existence of probable cause, or its companion "reasonable suspicion," may protect the merchant and private special police for their actions based on probable cause, but does not shield a private operative from liability for an arrest for an offense committed outside his presence. Such an arrest is beyond the private operative's authority and subjects him and his employer to a claim of false arrest—if he is wrong about whether a crime occurred or who perpetrated it. [7]

Excessive Force

"Excessive force" is more force than reasonably necessary to accomplish any lawful arrest, detainment, or compliance with a lawful order. Reasonable force is not a vague term: with very little difficulty, courts make the determination every day in every criminal court in the country. Reasonable force is enough force—but not a touch more—than is necessary under the circumstances to cause the suspect to yield to authority: so, when a show of force such as flashing a badge will suffice, using the baton is not justified. [8]

Malicious Prosecution

Whenever a suspect is criminally charged and is found not guilty, or at least the matter is resolved in his favor, a private operative and his employer are in serious jeopardy of a claim of malicious prosecution. If the suspect can prove malice, ill-will, spite, lack of probable cause, or "reckless and oppressive disregard of the {suspect's} rights," he has a viable case. [9]

Abuse of Process

When criminal or civil proceedings are used to extort, blackmail, or to cause the surrender of a legal right, the system has been corrupted; and the prosecution is thus used for a purpose other than intended by the law. The action lies when the proceeding is initiated legitimately enough, but thereafter some demand or threat is made which perverts the legal process. An example is an offer to drop criminal charges if a debt is paid. [10]

Defamation

There are enough varieties of defamation to warrant its own chapter (see **Defamation**, page 57). Suffice here to say that when security points a finger at a store customer and shouts for other customers to hear that he stole something, he'd better be right. [11]

Intentional Infliction of Emotional Distress

A strip search of a suspect, even when probable cause exists that a crime was committed, has great potential to inflict emotional distress. But so does a too-tight surveillance under the wrong circumstances. [12]

(See **Surveillance**, page 35)

Chapter 2 - Table of Authorities

1. *Rockwell v. Sun Harbor,* 925 P2d 1175 (Nev 1996).
2. *Lisa M. Henry Mayo,* 48 CalRptr2d 510 (Cal 1995).
3. *Hoover v. U. of Chicago,* 366 NE2d 925, 935 (Ill 1977).
4. *State v. Graham,* 927 P2d 227, 234 (Wash 1996).
5. *Roberts v. Benoit,* 605 So2d 1032 (La 1991).
6. *Murphy v. Army Distaff,* 458 A2d 61 (DC 1983).
7. *State v. Nall,* 404 SE2d 202 (SC 1990).
8. *State v. Beck,* 167 SW3d 767, 771 (Mo 2005).
9. *Bristow v. Clevenger,* 80 FSupp2d 421, 435 (MDPA 2000).
10. *Huggins v. Winn-Dixie,* 153 SE2d 693 (SC 1967).
11. *Manning v. Wexi,* 886 A2d 1137 (PA 2005).
12. *Kelly v. City of Minn.* 598 NW2d 657 (Minn 1999).

Chapter 3

Ruse, Impersonation, and Obstruction

"**Ruse**...*noun*...to dodge, deceive...a wily subterfuge... {a} trick."

Merriam-Webster's Collegiate Dictionary, Deluxe Edition, Merriam-Webster, Incorporated (1998).

3.1   INTRODUCTION

The detective steps up to the back door and rings the bell. The door opens a few inches and a young Hispanic looks out. "What's up?" At the painted table behind him sits the subject, maybe forty, blotchy round face and oily slicked black hair just like the description in the detective's coat pocket. The lawsuit says he can't walk or bend, and is in constant pain. All this the result of an un-witnessed slide off a roof doing a repair for the gumshoe's client.

"Speak English?" the detective asks. The boy at the door nods that he does.

"I'm a neighbor. Walking the dog, my wife lost her diamond ring—Polly, that's the dog, she did some business on your front lawn. The wife, she cleaned it, but may have lost the ring in the yard. It's worth a lot—mucho dollars—maybe several thousand. She's hysterical. Tell you what—I'll pay five-hundred dollar reward if you find it!" The boy looks to the subject who stirs approvingly. The detective says, "I'll need the phone number here so I can check back about it later." The boy gives the number; the detective thanks him, and leaves.

The gumshoe's car is already in position. He just has to walk to the car and man the camera. A few minutes later, a head pops out to make sure the coast is clear. The two hustle down the front stairs and begin searching the front yard for the diamond: plenty of bending, crawling, and raking, but no obvious sign of pain, and, of course, no ring. That night the detective calls the phone number and the boy answers. "Just wanted you to know my wife found the ring," the detective says. "But she wants to pay you folks for your time. She's generous that way...a little something for anybody who helped look. How many were there?"

A pause, then, "Four."

"Give me the names and social security numbers for the checks and I'll drop them off."

The names and socials are read off, including the subject's name teamed with the social security number of a deceased Colorado resident; and two names of other supposed participants also with socials of more deceased citizens. Four checks in the amount of twenty-five dollars each are delivered, one for each of the four with the socials provided. The checks clear, three signed in the same handwriting as that used on the subject's check. These checks along with the video are presented to the subject's attorney for perusal, accompanied by no verbal or written threat. None is needed. The claim is immediately dropped when the subject, through his attorney. realizes what may lie in wait for him if he pursues a fraudulent claim. He is a deserving victim of a lawful ruse—supported by a fair acting job.

Play-acting goes with the detective's job. There isn't a private detective long in the business who hasn't found it necessary to play someone he is not. Sooner or later he will find out how much Hollywood he has in him. And he better be good. There will be times his pretty face depends on it. There are a thousand stories in the city's streets, and private detectives have a front row seat to much of it: nasty business this, with the law not always on his side. As those in the business know first hand, a gumshoe has to keep his head in the game to stay legal.

Ruse, Impersonation, and Obstruction

Semantics

The courts use "ruse," "subterfuge," and "pretext" as interchangeable concepts, with ruse used as the most common catch-all. Any of them could be and are used to describe some action intended to deceive someone for a lawful purpose—a "wily subterfuge." On the contrary, "impersonation" describes some unauthorized use of a title, status, or occupation by the role player involved. Like ruse, an impersonation may be lawfully used. However, the term impersonation is most often used in conjunction with a specific criminal statute outlawing the unauthorized use of an occupation that requires a license or is government or law enforcement related.

3.2 RUSE

A dictionary draws no moral judgment whether a ruse, subterfuge, or pretext is legal or illegal; whereas, the private operative does: he confines his trickery strictly to lawful purposes. Since the active gumshoe uses one or another ruse on nearly a daily basis to gain entrance to some place he would otherwise most definitely not be invited, or to accomplish one of a myriad of other uses to which a ruse is applied, he has to work hard to stay legal. And work it is to use the ubiquitous ruse while remaining true to the laws of trespass and privacy invasion (See the **"Good Ruse,"** page 43, and the **"Bad Ruse,"** page 52), while avoiding the pitfalls surrounding the procurement of personal records. But it can be done and must be done if a detective is to stay in business.

In North Carolina, a private detective pulled off a typical ruse. Hired to find out if the other side of a lawsuit involving his client was abiding by a confidentiality agreement reached as part of the lawsuit settlement, the detective visited the other side's lawyer and play-acted he was a potential client with a similar case, presuming the lawyer would be in a mood to brag. When the lawyer found out he'd been duped, he sued. The court held the ruse perfectly lawful. [1]

Staying Legal

There is considerable authority that a gumshoe may law-fully use a ruse to accomplish a variety of lawful assign-ments. [2] For instance, a ruse is frequently used to gain entry to private property open to the public or at least semi-public; or to induce a person out of his house for the purpose of serving court process. [3] A lawful limit is reached, however, when the ruse invades private space, jeopardizes personal safety, or violates common sense. A detective knows better than to yell "fire" in a crowded movie theater to see if an allegedly disabled insurance claimant will toss his cane aside and scamper for the exit; or to place a telephone call to a relative of the subject claiming to be the emergency room doctor who needs vital medical information fast if he is to save the subject who has been involved in a terrible accident. [4] (See **Invasion of Privacy**, page 35)

Ruse to Procure Records

A detective encounters frequent client requests to procure the personal records of some third person. Most of these requests are rejected out of hand as obviously illegal: for instance, procuring official government records [5] or business trade secrets. [6] Some laws penalize the record keeper, not the detective, for illegal release: such as video rental records [7] and student records. [8] But the brunt of client requests will be for medical, financial, credit records and copies of tele-phone and e-mails. For the gumshoe, these records are spelled: t-r-o-u-b-l-e.

Medical Records

A ruse used to deceive a patient to get his authorization to procure his medical records or a ruse used to extract medical or psychiatric records from a doctor or an institution's medical personnel invades the patient's personal privacy; and entering a medical facility's restricted spaces for that purpose may well result in more than mere inconvenience. Federal and state laws universally protect the confidentiality of psychiatric and medical records. It is a safe and required course that the detective procures proper patient authorization before approaching a doctor or hospital for an individual's medical or psychiatric records. This is an instance where ruse will not work to negate a trespass; and exposes the detective to substantial civil damages and possible criminal charges. When an individual's medical condition is the subject of an investigation, usually a detective can procure authorization for the records through consent obtained by the applicable insurance company, or, in matters involving litigation, agreement of the attorneys. Meanwhile, of course, the detective is free to observe and record the public activities of the claimant to determine the veracity of any claimed disability or alleged medical findings.[9]

Financial Records

Federal law outlaws pretext to obtain unpublished personal information from a banker, financial institution, or financial customer. The law defines financial institutions broadly so think twice before spinning yarn to get personal information from a credit card company, personal banker, stock manager, a mortgage lender, or annuity-health insurance company. See *The Financial Services Modernization Act of 1999 (also known as The Gramm-Leach-Bliley Act), Public Law 106-102*. (See **Permissible Purpose**, page 39)

Credit Records

Credit information should also raise red flags when compiling a financial dossier for a client. A specific "permissible purpose" is required for a licensed detective to access an individual's credit report without the individual's consent. Procuring the report without a permissible purpose is a criminal offense under federal law. Permissible purposes include most legitimate investigative tasks. See *The Fair Credit Reporting Act (FCRA), 15 USC 1681, et seq.* (See **Permissible Purpose**, page 39)

DMV Records

Similarly, a detective must have a permissible purpose to lawfully access the data base of most states' motor vehicle departments. See *The Drivers' Privacy Protection Act, 18 U.S.C., Section 22 (a).* (See **Permissible Purpose**, page 39)

Telephone and E-Mail

The Telephone and Privacy Protection Act of 2006, 18 U.S.C. Sect. 1039 prohibits pretext to obtain confidential phone records and customer lists from an employee of the firm.

The content of e-mails are federally protected by *The Electronic Communications Privacy Act, 18 U.S.C. Sect. 2701 et seq.* (See **Eavesdropping**, page 75); but the identity of the holder of the e-mail address (like the holder of a private unlicensed telephone number) is not. When the name is provided on the application for service, privacy is lost. [10]

3.3 IMPERSONATION

A simple change in persona to gain investigative advantage is an important tool in any gumshoe's repertoire. Playing a fictional movie producer in town checking sites for an upcoming film has been known to literally open a door or two. But an experienced gumshoe also knows there are some false impressions he cannot make or he risks running afoul of the law. Specifically, certain occupations and government affiliations are off the table; and misleading police can make things dicey. [11]

Falsely Claiming License or Occupation

Federal Statutes

It is unlawful to impersonate *and* exercise the authority of a federal employee in an effort to acquire anything of value or to seek some financial advantage. The federal statute involved, *Impersonation of a Federal Official, 18 U.S.C. Section 912,* provides:

> Whoever falsely assumes or pretends to be an officer or employee acting under the authority of the United States or any department, agency or officer thereof, and acts as such, or in such pretended manner character demands or obtains any money, paper, document or thing of value, shall be (fined or imprisoned)....

In the 7ᵗʰ Circuit, a speeder was federally prosecuted for passing himself off as a U.S. marshal. When stopped by a local traffic cop, he said he was on his way to break up a bar fight. The officer didn't believe him. He got out of the ticket but was indicted for impersonating a government employee. On appeal, the court held he broke the law, not when he said he was a marshal, but rather when he exercised authority claiming he was on official duty. Also, his purpose was clearly financial, attempting to avoid a traffic citation. [12]

State Laws

State laws prohibit impersonation of police and licensed professionals such as doctors, lawyers, and, among others, of course, private detectives. These statutes do not always require evidence of an attempt at financial gain. Just using the impersonation is a statutory violation.

> *In Kansas,* on television, an author puffed his new book claiming he was a lawyer when in fact he was not. He was prosecuted and earned a year in jail to do more writing. [13]

> *In Texas,* a part-time bail bondsman, full-time hog farmer, came off his ranch long enough to ask local police for their help in nabbing a bond fugitive. To ensure they'd tag along, he claimed to be a fellow deputy from another county. But police concluded he didn't look much like a deputy: his shirt was ripped and boots smeared with what looked like blood; and he smelled like he'd stepped in something. He finished the day in jail and was ultimately convicted of impersonating a public servant. [14]

> *In Illinois,* it is a felony to impersonate a host of active and inactive officials, including police retirees, members of a police fraternal association, and even representatives of certain charitable organizations. (See, *720 ILCS 5/17-2)*

There is an inclination of regular police to take a close look at any security officer spotted off-site in a police-like uniform, with police-like badge, driving a police-like squad-car.

In Illinois, a security guard with a clip board and uniform was written up by local police as imper-sonating one of their own when he strayed from his employer's mall. The cop examined the badge and insignia on the car and thought they were too close to regular police. The court tossed the case, noting the private security guard was properly dressed in uniform with security badge and vehicle appropriate to his duties and there was no law which said security police could not leave their employer's property so long as they did not exercise police authority when doing so. [15]

Misleading Police to Get Information

A client may have good, lawful reasons for keeping his name out of it when he sends his hired gun forth to see what police will tell him about a pending matter. Usually the gumshoe will make every lawful effort to accommodate since he has no legal requirement to make things easy for police. Why should he cough up his client's name just because the duty officer asks who is he working for? Of course, he can refuse to answer, but that diplomacy will get a lot less than just telling the cop a phony story with a straight face. But is he breaking any law when he does so? Specifically, is he obstructing justice?

Obstruction of a Police Officer

It is criminal obstruction to intentionally take steps which prevent an officer from performing his official investigative duties. But the cases are consistent that the intention involved requires more than merely giving false information when one is not a suspect in the crime under investigation. Certainly, where the person questioned is even under reasonable suspicion, the minimum standard, as in a Terry stop, the outcome may be different.

In Iowa, the word "obstruct" means an actual hindrance of official duties; that is, doing some act that actually hinders the officer in his immediate investigation or performance of duties. An example might be lying down in front of a police car to keep the officer from doing his job. [16]

In Illinois, the Illinois statute was used as a basis to convict a traffic offender of obstruction when he used a false name to throw off a police computer scan of his prior record. [17]

Likewise, *in Colorado,* courts found an individual guilty of obstruction for giving police a false identity during a traffic stop. [18]

In Wisconsin, a non-suspect witness charged with obstruction for refusing to cooperate with police and provide information he had was found not guilty; his refusal to give police correct information about himself in of itself did not constitute conduct that obstructed the officer. This person was questioned in a private place and the court indicated results might be different if it had been a Terry stop in a public place. [19]

And, again in *Illinois,* the Illinois Supreme Court said, "{The obstruction} statute...requires more than giving of false information...it requires that when the false information is given, it must be given with the intent to prevent the prosecution...." [20]

Before employing a tactic of this type, giving police a false client name or story as to why information is needed, the private eye must check local application of his state's obstruction statute.

Providing False Personal Identification

There is considerable case authority that an individual can change his name at any time without asking anyone's permission. [21] Working by that rule means a private detective

31

will often use a pseudonym for bona fide investigative pur-poses—*provided* there exists no licensing regulation which might specifically prohibit use of a false name by a private detective, the action does not tread into protected privacy, or does not violate a broadly construed impersonation statute such as those which prohibit any "benefit" from use of the false name. Arguably, "benefit" is vague and just too broad a term to say categorically it does not include a private detective seeking information from police. There is no case authority for guidance on the point to say the gumshoe is not breaking the law so the practice is best avoided entirely. [22]

 Warning A confusing mix of statutes regarding imper-sonation and use of other names poses a quandary for any private detective who misdirects the public or police in an effort to gather intelligence without disclosing his or his client's real interest.

In summary:

- No private detective should claim he is part of law enforcement, a government employee, or that he pos-sesses a professional license he does not in fact have.
- When dealing with *police*, vis-à-vis the general public, a private detective should not misidentify *himself.*
- When dealing with police, on-site judgment or local application of obstruction laws may overrule case authority—which provides no compelling legal reason that either a false *client name* or *reason* cannot be used in seeking information.

Chapter 3 - Table of Authorities

1. *Keyzer v. Amerlink,* 618 SE2d 768 (NC 2005).

2. *Desnick v. ABC,* 44 F3d 1345 (7th Cir 1995).

3. *People v. Sunday,* 441 NE2d 374, 378 (Ill 1982).

4. *Taus v. Loftus,* 151 P3d 1185, 1221 (Cal 2007).

5. *U.S. v. DiGilio,* 538 F2d 972 (3rd Cir 1976).

6. *USA v. Yang,* 281 F3d 534, 541 (9th Cir 2002).

7. *Daniel v. Cantrell,* 375 F3d 377, 384 (6th Cir 2004).

8. *Gonzaga University v. Doe,* 2002 SCt 129 (US 2002).

9. *Mann v. University of Cincinnati,* 824 FSupp 1190 (Ohio 1993).

10. *U.S. v. Kennedy,* 81 FSupp2d 1103, 1110 (DKan 2000).

11. *Alvarado v. People,* 132 P3d 1205 (Colo 2006).

12. *U.S. v. Rippe,* 961 F2d 677 (7th Cir 1992).

13. *State v. Marino,* 929 P2d 173, 176 (Kan 1996).

14. *Dietz v. State,* 62 SW3d 335 (Tex 2001).

15. *People v. Rinehart,* 225 NE2d 486 (Ill App 1967).

16. *State v. Henley,* 2001 IA 61 (IACA 2001).

17. *People v. Remias,* 523 NE2d 1106, 1108 (Ill 1988).

18. *State v. Johnson,* 30 P3d 718 (Colo 2000).

19. *People v. Hamilton,* 356 NW2d 169 (Wi 1984).

20. *People v. Gray,* 496 NE2d 1269, 1271 (Ill 1986).

21. *People v. Jones,* 376 NYS2d 885 (NYSup 1975).

22. *Alvarado v. People,* 132 P3d 1205, 1209 (Colo 2006).

Chapter 4

Surveillance: Stalking, Trespass, and Invasion of Privacy

{S}talkers, in seeking to locate and track a victim, sometimes use an investigator to obtain personal information about the victims...The threats posed by stalking and identity theft lead us to conclude that the risk of criminal misconduct is sufficiently foreseeable so that an investigator has a duty to exercise reasonable care in disclosing a third person's personal information to a client. *Remsberg v. Docusearch, Inc.*, 816 A2d 1001, 1007-1008 (NH 2003).

4.1 INTRODUCTION

Every private detective hopes his work that day goes undetected; that he tags his quarry to destination; gets pictures; then breaks off without being made. But hope won't make this surveillance any different than most: hope won't control the driving habits of his target; or whether that day's subject meets his lover in public or behind closed doors; and hope certainly won't stop his client from telling the target that very morning she was on to him and would have a private detective watching him.

So this day the hapless gumshoe picks him after work and struggles to follow the blue Buick in rush-hour traffic. If he gets too far behind, he risks another car blocking him at the changing light; if he gets too close, the target may get to know him in the rear view mirror, or they might even make eye contact—effectively terminating the surveillance. After about thirty minutes of this grueling drill, he can't honestly say whether he's been burned or not. The guy seems oblivious. Or is it a set-up? He knows all too well that many a detective has followed a car into a dead-end street only to find the supposedly unaware target waiting for him.

In this instance, the Buick pulls into a restaurant parking lot and the detective parks across the street, to wait and see. He must anticipate the Buick might come right back out, so the dick takes a spot and waits. In his mirror he can see the man enter the restaurant, so it's time to change hats, get the camera bag, and follow him in. It is risky to get this close, but that is what he gets paid for.

Our detective acts oblivious to the target and the young woman he has joined in a booth, takes an open seat directly across the room, and sets the bag with pager camera attached on the table. He orders a sandwich for show and uses the waitress to shield him while he gets the lens just right to catch their hands touching under the table. Probably all he'll get for now, so he'll grab a bite, then go outside to pick up her plate number and follow *her* when she leaves. He'll learn all he can about her. Women are much easier to follow, anyway.

His sandwich arrives, but he notices the guy is glancing over way too much. Suddenly, the subject loosens his tie and stands up. He's taller and more muscular than the detective first realized. The detective tries to remember if the little health insurance policy he took out is current. The man walks over to the dick's table and looks down, feet spread, thumbs hooked in his belt. He does not look happy.

"You following me?"

The detective looks up: he's calm, has to be, and fiddles with the ketchup bottle—but not for his sandwich. "Yeah, matter of fact, I was—you cut me off at Cicero and Diversey."

"What?"

"Nearly put me in the curb. I wanted your plate number." He gestures to the girl across the room. "See now why you were in such a hurry."

The target shrugs, "I don't remember doing that. Sorry, man, sorry."

"Aw, let it go." The detective looks at his sandwich and applies ketchup. "I'm hungry, anyway."

The subject returns to his booth and the detective finishes the sandwich, pays and leaves. He's got pictures and the surveillance is over for today. Further surveillance might mean another confrontation and at this point a broken nose, or a claim of harassment, or invasion of privacy, or maybe all three. He'll pick it up later, with a different car, maybe a disguise; but today—he's done. Still, a decent day's work—he now knows there is someone else—more than half the battle. The rest is patience and money. He has enough now to make the client game, and he'll get them later, another time, another place: the goods, the pictures, the works.

Any experienced private detective knows the margin of error is slight in the unforgiving world of spying on someone in close quarters. In a single day—on a single surveillance— a detective may see his personal estate evaporate, his personal freedom lost to claims of stalking, trespass, or invasion of privacy, or he may be physically assaulted. Surveillance is a test of his ability to stay legal while getting the goods.

And the law does not make it easy. Stalking, trespass, and invasion of privacy are all separately actionable and flow from close and intense surveillance.

4.2   STALKING

Even with all the tricks he can muster, there are times when the gumshoe gets too close to his target. Sometimes it seems their vehicles are the only two on the road and he can only mutter, "Where have all the cars gone?" Among other concerns: his state's stalking law. Every state now has an anti-stalking law (oft referred to as "stalking" or expanded to "harassment" to cover threatening phone calls and letters). These laws come into play when undertaking an intense personal surveillance. Stalking laws are intended to prevent surveillance that places a person in reasonable apprehension of bodily harm. Picture the mindset of a female driver when she realizes a beat-up SUV with Marine Corps Semper Fi emblems pasted to every window has been following her for ten miles. A busy detective is often so close to his target that he forgets he may be putting the person he is following in fear of her life. A tight surveillance can prompt a cell call to police and the gumshoe may soon find himself being tailed—by a cruiser with Mars lights. Rarely is the detective exempt from the state's stalking laws. He can't just flash his credentials and go on his way. In most states, the state does not want the detective "stalking by proxy"; that is, tailing a person to follow the target to get her address simply to save the client the trouble; so the client can then go out and kill her. The law requires there be some lawful purpose to the tail. A detective does not just go out and follow someone or just get their address or learn their habits. What is the reason we need to know this information?

> *In New Hampshire,* a private eye claimed his license alone gave him immunity from prosecution when he followed his target closely and too often—a possible violation of his state's stalking law. The court disagreed:
>
> The {detective} had to do more than merely testify he was a licensed private detective who was hired to follow the plaintiff. He also had to show the purpose for which he was hired was itself lawful. For instance, had he been hired to follow the plaintiff so that a third person could kill her, the purpose for which he was hired, then, was not lawful. [1]

There is wide variance amongst the states in how surveillance actions of a private detective are treated under his state's stalking law:

- It is a rare state which exempts the detective based on his license alone;
- In others
  - while not exempt, he is excused if he proves he had a lawful purpose; or
  - the detective has an affirmative defense—after being charged—that the surveillance had a lawful purpose; or
  - the detective cannot be charged until there has been at least two separate incidences which he cannot prove had "lawful justification."

Surveillance: Stalking, Trespass, and Invasion of Privacy

Talk about a situation in which a gumshoe must check state laws! The bottom line is that in almost every such situation, the detective must cooperate with police, prosecutor, and, if it goes that far, the judge; and be prepared to disclose his lawful purpose.

Lawful Purpose

What is lawful purpose? One way to answer is that after "reasonable care" in evaluating the client's request for a tail the detective verifies the requested investigation will *not* be for a criminal purpose; [2] and otherwise complies with his statutory authority to investigate the "habits, conduct, business occupation, honesty, integrity...movements, whereabouts...(and) acts...of any person, firm, association or occupation." (See the Illinois sample statute, *The Private Detective and Private Security Act of 1993, 225 ILCS 446/5)*

"GUMSHOE" TIP

Since a neighbor's call to police may result in the gumshoe confronted by men in blue while in close proximity to his subject—a potentially compromising development—the wise detective finds it advisable to call police dispatch in advance of a planned stake-out, providing just enough general detail to establish his surveillance is lawful: that the purpose of the stake-out or moving surveillance is to comply with his statutory authority. Police desk personnel have a calming way with people who call 911 to complain of a beater car with a man in sunglasses parked in their neighborhood all day.

Permissible Purpose

To do his job a private detective uses the DMV and credit bureaus for unpublished personal data including home and work addresses, socials, drivers' license numbers, telephone numbers, and car plate numbers of the subject and other involved parties. To lawfully access this personal data he provides data providers with his legitimate investigative purpose for that particular investigation—called his "permissible purpose."

A problem arises, however, when his client puts him in the proverbial trick bag—by demanding the non-published personal information directly from the gumshoe without providing an appropriate permissible purpose. In effect, he asks the detective to merely re-sell the personal information. That tactic comes with a host of baggage.

First and foremost, there is a duty owed the public by the private detective to use reasonable care not to subject third persons to an unreasonable risk. Giving raw personal data of a third person to an unknown client or one without an ostensible need to know may court disaster. The recipient of such information may well be a potential stalker—or worse! In 1989 a crazed fan killed actress Rebecca Schaeffer using an address provided by a private detective for a $225 fee. In effect, the detective got the address for a lesser sum and just resold the starlet's address to the killer. The killer provided no bona fide investigative need to know the home address of the victim. As a result of this breakdown in what sometimes amounted to an honor system, the federal government has since passed *The Drivers' Privacy Protection Act of 1994 ("DPPA"), 18 U.S.C. Section 2721-2724,* to regulate access to DMV information.

The *DPPA*'s regulatory scheme and state application in most cases strives to direct the flow of personal information to the right people for the right reasons. Likewise, under *The Financial Services Modernization Act of 1999*, also known as *The Gramm-Leach-Bliley Act, Public Law 106-112;* and *The Fair Credit Reporting Act, 15 U.S.C., Section 1681 et seq.,* financial and credit bureau access to personal data has similar constraints. Each act provides heavy penalties for any detective providing raw personal information to a client or third person without permissible purpose.

Surveillance: Stalking, Trespass, and Invasion of Privacy

Warning

The long list of authorized permissible purposes available to a private detective ensures there is no problem in finding one to fit any bona fide investigative situation. [3] The request of a client to find a long-lost girlfriend and to provide her address is, however, always a "how does it smell?" dilemma for any detective. In the justifiably security consciousness of the day, diligence is demanded before a gumshoe releases any non-published personal data to anyone. In most cases, where personal data is sought based on a past relationship, the detective advises his client he will call the third person involved first, ensuring the relationship exists. If the client backs off, so should the detective. He's now on notice that should he proceed, and a third person is harassed, or worse, his lack of diligence may be an issue in any subsequent civil or criminal investigation. [4]

4.3   TRESPASS

Although the two are closely tied, the issue we analyze here is not the intrusion into the subject's right to privacy caused by a physical trespass onto his property, but rather the criminal penalties or civil damages which result from the trespass itself. Trespass is usually defined as entering or remaining on the property of another without authority. The word "authority" is critical to the discussion since its presence may negate the offense. While trespass is a wholly separate offense from invasion of privacy, when trespass takes the private detective into the subject's private space, the offense counts heavily in assessing damages arising from an invasion of privacy. [5]

Living Space

No prior warning to stay out is requisite to finding trespass into a residence, curtilage, apartment dwelling, hotel room, or trailer used as a residence. Unlike police who are permitted very limited use of a ruse to enter a private residence under some circumstances, [6] a ruse to enter living quarters is never recommended for private operatives since most courts hold that any purpose other than the purpose for which entry was granted exceeds the scope of consent; thus, a meter reading ruse to get into living quarters when the actual purpose is to investigate is a trespass (and may itself support liability for invasion of privacy). A ruse to enter a private place includes change in "identity, calling, character, or other quality of the actor (and is) misrepresentation as to a material fact." [7]

Walkways

By custom and usage, unless the homeowner manifests by gates or signs to the contrary, there is implied invitation to use walkways, causeways, sidewalks, and other access routes to and from the home's entrance. [8] It is neither a trespass nor a violation of the disorderly conduct statute to use the walkway unless the occupant signals otherwise. But circumstances can affect this rule: a detective using the walkway late at night may find custom and usage has withdrawn the invitation except to those given specific permission to enter.[9]

Non-living Space

With respect to non-living space, specifically public or semi-public places, such as offices, industrial property, and the like, many states require proof of prior warning, whether verbal or by signage, before finding an interference with ownership or possession of property sufficient to support a trespass charge. [10]

> *In Illinois,* the state's *Damage and Trespass* statute requires just such a warning: "Whoever: (1) knowingly and without lawful authority enters or remains within or on a building; or (2) enters upon the land of another, *after receiving, prior to such entry, notice* from the owner or occupant that such entry is forbidden; or remains upon the land of another, after receiving notice from the owner or occupant to depart...commits a Class B misdemeanor." (See, *720 ILCS 5/21-3) (emphasis provided).* The statute also

> provides that trespass does not apply to being in a building "which is open to the public while the building is open to the public during its normal hours of operation"; nor does it apply to a person who enters a building under the reasonable belief that the building is open to the public.

Thus public or private property open to public or semi-public use is generally accessible directly or by ruse unless the entry is contrary to a lawful order not to enter or in defiance of an order to get out when such order is personally communicated by a person in authority. But this open-faced license to enter public or semi-public use property does not justify entry into a non-public or restricted portion of any building, either clearly posted or known to be off-limits by virtue of prior warnings, markings, custom, usage, or some "clear and present danger." A gumshoe knows he cannot walk in the back door of a currency exchange or slip by the guard at a nuclear plant. No warning is necessary. [11] And claiming he was lost, won't work. [12]

> *In New York*, protesters got permission to enter a newsroom during a live broadcast by ruse that they were college students there to observe. The room was clearly guarded and off-limits to the public. When they demonstrated during the live show, they were arrested and subsequently convicted of trespass. [13]

The "Good" Ruse

A "good" ruse may avoid trespass charges. By good ruse is meant a cover which, when things go wrong and security is alerted, has the gumshoe escorted off the property, not to a squad car. A good ruse works because the building or property is at least semi-public, providing the detective has *not* had prior warning to stay out, and the property is not restricted by virtue of custom or some clear and present danger. Easing into a company outing playing a photographer is an example of a good ruse that works because the event is at least semi-public and the property, unless posted or there has been prior warning to stay out, is not restricted by custom or clear and present danger. Obviously, when a ruse is "blown," the detective is ordered out, and he immediately leaves, to not personally return. He has gotten his single warning. If there is another try, it will be by another detective.

> ## "GUMSHOE" TIP
>
> It is personal experience that when a ruse is exposed the detective is ejected; when a trespass is exposed, police are called. When in doubt, use a good ruse!

Consistent with case authority on the subject, consent to enter property open to the public, even if only semi-public, such as a banquet hall closed to the general public for a private event, social club, country club, law office, business office, restaurant, or any property or business establishment with some public contact, may be obtained through use of a good ruse, rendering such access lawful. [14]

In the 7th Circuit, the court reminded the parties that "the law's willingness to give effect to consent procured by fraud is not limited to the tort of trespass" and cited consent to sexual intercourse based on false promises, is excused by the law. A quiet reminder, perhaps, that even the court tips its hat to a good ruse, though obviously some are better than others. [15]

4.4   PEEPING TOM STATUTES

A Peeping Tom is a person who sneaks up to a house to look in the windows. [16] Even a private detective can't do that!—no, *especially* a private detective can't do that! Some state statutes call it disorderly conduct but all universally prohibit such conduct; and violators are criminally prosecuted. Some states require lewd purpose before the charge is applicable, but in most others, simply trespassing onto private residential property to look into the windows will do.

> *In Mississippi,* a court put it this way: A 'Peeping Tom' might be 'disorderly Tom.' Peeking into the window of an occupied residence or apartment at an hour of the night when occupants are likely to be preparing to retire...constitutes disorderly conduct within the terms of statutes and ordinances defining the offense as indecent or insulting conduct. [17]

> *In Louisiana,* no unlawful purpose is necessary to be declared a Peeping Tom. See Louisiana statute *LSA-R.S.14:284*: 'Peeping Tom' as used in this Section means one who peeps through windows or doors, or other like places, situated on or about the premises of another for the purpose of spying upon or invading the privacy of persons spied upon without the consent of the persons spied upon. It is not a necessary element of this offense that the 'Peeping Tom' be upon the premises of the person being spied upon.

4.5   INVASION OF PERSONAL PRIVACY

The right of privacy takes two forms: (1) the constitutional right against government intrusion into a person's reasonable expectation of privacy, usually resulting in the exclusion of evidence illegally obtained; and (2) tort remedies for injuries from invasion of personal privacy. The tort remedies are usually left to the states unless there is government participation, in which case federal remedies are available to help compensate. There are various forms of invasion, some or all adopted by most of the states. These forms include appropriation of one's name or likeness, publicity that places the individual in a false light, public disclosure of private personal facts, and intrusion upon a person's seclusion, solitude or private affairs. Of these branches, the latter, intrusion, comes directly into the operative's wheelhouse when he intrudes "physically or otherwise," upon the solitude of another person in a manner "highly offensive to a *reasonable person.*" [18]

The Reasonable Person

In claims of invasion of personal privacy, courts strive to level the playing field between the investigator's duty to get facts (a societal interest) and the investigated party's effort to withhold facts (his personal privacy interest). The referee in this constant struggle is the omnipresent *reasonable person.* Once again the hapless gumshoe is put into an unenviable position. He must find an invisible line in the sand and not cross it or he will offend the reasonable person. Fortunately, there is enough uniformity amongst the various state courts to discern some patterns of good and safe rules of what offends the reasonable person. [19]

Elements of Invasion of Privacy

When does the detective's conduct offend the sensibilities of the reasonable person? When does he intrude into the privacy of the reasonable person?

The privacy invasion tort, often referred to as the "intrusion upon seclusion tort," consists of four elements:

1) An unauthorized intrusion or prying into the plaintiff's private space (his solitude and seclusion);
2) the intrusion was offensive to a reasonable person;
3) the matter intruded into is private; and
4) the intrusion caused anguish and suffering. [20]

General Privacy Rules

Any detective who watches his target for a few days waiting for a single event to occur and then is lucky enough to see that very event unfold, knows this is no time to dilly-dally and it's too late to try and remember the elements of invasion of privacy. That's for lawyers to study at their desks with the door closed. Say, for example, he follows his subject to a secluded beach with a woman not his wife and can film them taking a roll in the sand. The moment he has waited for has arrived! But now he hesitates—he lowers his camera as a thought crosses his mind: if he snaps the picture he might be sued for a million dollars—not by his subject; no fear there because he has a legitimate reason to investigate the husband—no, his fear is of a claim by the woman that he invaded *her* privacy. Just visualizing that many zeros on a page opposite his name is enough for any gumshoe to pass on any picture taking and call it a day. How then can a private eye who works for a pittance do his job if he has to continually worry about losing his house by offending someone's privacy? By the very nature of his calling, he watches people on most every caper do things they want kept private—usually *very* private.

He shouldn't worry so much. While no detective can ever totally immunize himself from frivolous lawsuits; he can protect himself from bona fide claims by following a few simple rules gleaned from countless court decisions of most every jurisdiction (not to say there are not a few contrary opinions lying in wait somewhere in the fifty states).

In a nutshell, he should remember six simple rules:

Rule 1: What the subject does in the *public eye* is not protected;

Rule 2: Don't *trespass* private places;

Rule 3: Don't *scope* a private place;

Rule 4: Don't use the *bad ruse*;

Rule 5: Don't delve into *irrelevant* matters;

Rule 6: Don't make a *pest* of yourself.

Rule 1: **What the Subject Does in the *Public Eye* Is Not Protected**

In our beach scenario the detective had it easy. Secluded beach or not, the tort of invasion of privacy does not apply to activities in the public eye. If done in public, there is no privacy to be intruded upon and the issue generally ends there. [21] The law does not require the private detective confine his observations to only those instances where some third person conveniently strolls by. If the activity can be observed by a third person from a place he has a right to be, whether the third person is present or not, the activity is in the *public eye*—be it a single member of the public or a group which does not include the gumshoe—it is still the public eye: trespass in itself does not make a view unreasonable. On the other hand, courts have found enough seclusion to warrant privacy protection in the subject's dwelling, or other like reclusive location, such as his hospital room, an ambulance in which he was rushed to the hospital, and a doctor's office. In all these cases the intruder entered a private place where the public eye has been tightly excluded; where "an ordinary man in the plaintiff's position could reasonably expect that the particular defendant should be excluded." [22]

What then about a closed party, when the door is locked to the public, with only invited guests permitted in by pass only? Can our gumshoe slip in and film a marital cheater with his girlfriend? Is there a third person who qualifies as a member of the public present? Undoubtedly so!

> *In Maryland,* a gumshoe got past the gate to a closed to non-members, invitation only, boat club to film the supposedly disabled insurance claimant doing hard physical labor on his boat. The court applauded the detective's ruse to get in the club and his efforts at exposing the insurance fraud. "The {subject} was performing acts which were in public view to other members of the club...{hardly}...an intrusion of Plaintiff's right to seclusion." [23]

Surveillance: Stalking, Trespass, and Invasion of Privacy

Rule 2: Don't *Trespass* Private Places

Normally, trespassing onto private property does not prove or disprove an invasion of privacy. Trespass onto a neighbor's property to look over at the subject's property is not encouraged; but if the view is open to the public anyway, the trespass is immaterial and has no bearing on the outcome. But when the trespass hands the detective a view not observable by the public—say, the subject's private place of seclusion—his residence, curtilage, private office, apartment, hotel room (note: listening from an adjoining hotel room with the natural ear is *not* physical intrusion—See, **Public Ear**, Page 77) or other private space of seclusion—the trespass has crossed the line: the gumshoe is now—by virtue of trespass—viewing something he and the public are not entitled to see. Whatever he gets by this venture is bound to be an aggravating factor in any subsequent invasion of privacy, and, in itself, may constitute invasion of privacy. [24]

And while we can say that "trespass alone cannot automatically change an otherwise reasonable surveillance into an unreasonable one," [25] we must add that if trespass enhances the detective's view into the subject's private place beyond what he can see from a place he has a right to be, the court will smite him. This is the difference in whether the surveillance was okay or "highly offensive to a reasonable man." [26]

Rule 3: Don't *Scope* a Private Place

Use of binoculars, telescopes, and high-powered camera zoom lens to view the interior of a private place, such as dwelling or curtilage, even from a location on the public street, may constitute invasion of privacy. The magnified view may reach into an area of the dwelling the occupant reasonably expects is private, a private space which cannot be seen without the scope.

The starting point is that a gumshoe or police officer may use natural eyesight to observe and videotape what he can see from a place he has a right to be. If the subject can be viewed from there and he objects, he should close the drapes. [27] Thus, using a telescope to watch someone in the window of his house from a vantage point a mile away is lawful if the observer could see the same thing with his natural eyesight at the lot line. The glass has merely brought the view closer.

In the 2nd Circuit, the court put it this way:

If in his home he conducts activities or places objects in such a way that the activities or objects are seen by unenhanced viewing of persons outside the home, located where they may properly be, such observations transgress no Fourth Amendment protection because 'no intention...has been exhibited' by the householder to prevent the unenhanced viewing of others...Absent exposure to such unenhanced viewing, however, we do not believe the inference of intended privacy at home is rebutted by a failure to obstruct telescopic viewing by closing the curtains. [28]

In Washington, a state whose constitution is even broader in privacy protection than that provided by U.S. Constitution's Fourth Amendment, a court explained the parameters of the use of binoculars:

{Use} of binoculars does not constitute a particularly intrusive method of viewing so long as the object observed could have been seen with the naked eye had the officer been closer to it...{W}hat is voluntarily exposed to the general public and observable without the use of enhancement devices from an unprotected area is not considered part of a person's private affairs. [29]

The problem arises when scopes are used to magnify what the natural eyesight can not see if closer; what the natural eye is capable of seeing from the street or property line does not include the inner reaches of a house: it is no exaggeration that a scope can easily make readable a prescription bottle on a kitchen counter. [30]

In Louisiana, two accident investigators used binoculars to "peep" into the window of the home of their subject. Generally, what a detective can see with the naked eye is fair game, even in the innards of a home, provided the view is from a public area. While a householder must be prepared to assume the risk that activities inside the house may be observed from persons in the street using the naked eye, he is not prepared for someone using binoculars. [31]

Thus, use of binoculars, telescopes, and high-powered camera zoom lens to view the interior of the subject's private place, be it his dwelling, curtilage, or other private space, even from a location on the public street, may constitute invasion of privacy for the private eye (and potential Fourth Amendment violation for the police officer). If the magnified view enhances what a sleuth can see from a place he has a right to be, into an area the occupant reasonably believes is secluded, his privacy is invaded.

As to the curtilage itself—a unique area: open, yet private—an area determined by its proximity to the house, the use to which it is put, and steps taken to preserve privacy—an enhanced view into this area is off-limits if the occupant has taken steps to protect his privacy in such space. To ensure seclusion, a tall fence will do, but signs will not. [32] Then too, because the intrusion is considered temporary and minimal, courts have approved an aircraft fly-over at a lawful altitude. [33]

In summary, when a scope is used to delve into an area reasonably believed by a person to be private, which cannot be seen with natural eyesight from a place the viewer has a right to be, there is potential for invasion of personal privacy and Fourth Amendment violation if police are involved.

In the 11th Circuit, the court held that "the use of vision-enhancing devices can taint an otherwise valid surveillance of the interior of a home, when the devices allow the observer to view, not only activities the homeowner should realize might be seen by unenhanced viewing, but also details of activities the homeowner legitimately expects not to be observed." [34]

There are also those situations in which the subject makes the decision easy, by displaying an obvious disregard of his privacy rights; making his claim of privacy unreasonable.

> *In Oregon,* police were called to investigate a subject in his house exposing himself to passers-by in the street. There had been numerous sightings of the activity and police used a camera with a 135 MM zoom to get his picture. His conviction for indecent exposure was upheld by the court which justified the use of the magnification as irrelevant. The court held the subject did not seek privacy for his actions. [35]

Magnified View

How much magnification renders the view invasive? There is authority that an off-the-shelf camera with accompanying zoom presents no "sophisticated gadgetry" or "special equipment not generally in use." [36] Such minor magnification presents no particular privacy issues, but courts go no further: use of the binocular and telescope has drawn the ire of courts. These devices can rival those used in a ship's crow's nest. [37] The magnified view is an invaluable tool for the detective; but should be confined to areas other than private space. These devices should not be used to photograph or log a privacy invasion. (See **Camera Zoom**, page 87)

Rule 4: Don't Use the *Bad Ruse*

A "bad ruse" is a misrepresentation that breaches personal privacy by intruding into private space. Courts readily accept the ruse in many instances—usually those involving an entry into a public or semi-public property or event, where the public eye rides along; but courts do not accept a gumshoe's misrepresentation to get into the subject's private place. Thus, any story other than the truth to get entrance into a dwelling, curtilage, or his other private space sanctuary is a potential fraudulent misrepresentation and invasion of privacy. Although some courts have accepted ruse by police to gain consent to enter a residence, for an otherwise lawful purpose, this process has also drawn considerable fire and is something a private operative must avoid.

> *In Illinois*, a private investigator got entrance into a residence claiming he was looking for a missing young girl. In actuality, he wanted to secretly video the homeowner who had filed an insurance disability claim. When he testified later in a workmen's compensation case as to what he observed, he was in turn sued for invasion of privacy. The court agreed he had violated the subject's privacy. [38]

Rule 5: Don't Delve into *Irrelevant* Matters

A private detective must keep his eye on the ball. As an example, going undercover and posing as a fellow employee to investigate store thefts, he must not branch his investigation into personal matters unrelated to the matter at hand. The gratuitous reporting of irrelevant matter, such as employee family matters, romantic interests, future employment plans, and complaints about management, likely invades the employee's privacy and is actionable as invasion of privacy. [39]

Rule 6: Don't Make a *Pest* of Yourself

We're not through with invasion of privacy. Courts recognize one's right to conduct his affairs free of harassment; the "right to be left alone"—the right to be free of intense and obvious surveillance. Under this authority, a detective's actions are offensive to a reasonable person when he follows his quarry too closely, and, too often, blatantly. In short, the detective is a pest; his surveillance tactics so blatant and persistent that the subject is justified in making claim that he is under siege, perhaps in physical danger. Under this line of cases a detective or crew of detectives hound a subject for extended periods at close range; perhaps look in house windows, or set up shop outside his house to ensure neighbors know he is under surveillance; or chase his car at perilously close range; or all of the above. Such surveillance tactics invariably come to no good end. The detective should sense he has sorely tested a reasonable person's sensibilities. [40]

Chapter 4*In Georgia,* two detectives repeatedly stayed on the subject's tail as she drove to the store. The surveillance was obvious, prolonged and harassing. The court held the conduct of the detectives highly offensive to a reasonable person. The right to investigate does not include "overt and prolonged 'trailing'...in a conspicuous manner sufficient to excite the speculation of neighbors, constant following in public places, pursuit tactics openly conducted late at night such as would ordinarily alarm an average person." [41]

The lawful authority of the gumshoe to observe and determine "activity, movements and whereabouts of persons" is always subject to a qualification: almost every state prohibits activities which amount to harassment. A good detective knows that a failed mission must be accepted as part of the job. In that context, he will have many failed missions. [42]

"GUMSHOE" TIP

Since the object of surveillance is not to be seen, a private detective who is repeatedly burned is doing something wrong—perhaps he should lose some weight, drop the fedora for a baseball cap, or throttle back both himself and his vehicle. There is always another day if he backs off when it becomes obvious he is spotted. There may not be another day, however, if he continues the surveillance and violence erupts and someone is injured or charges are levied. Every detective on every mission has potential for just such a scrum—because he is dealing with the unpredictability of the most complicated and devious computer on earth—his subject.

54

Chapter 4 - Table of Authorities

1. *Miller v. Blackden,* 913 A2d 742, 748 (NH 2006).

2. *Miller v. Blackden,* 913 A2d 742 (NH 2006).

3. Compilation summary of typical data provider's list of permissible purposes per 18 U.S.C. Sect. 2721 (b): investigations complying with federal state, and local laws, rules and other applicable legal requirements; insurance matters; collection matters; subpoena and summons by federal, state, and local authorities; due diligence—to prevent fraud; law enforcement matters; any use reasonably expected as part of the normal course and scope of business or profession.

4. *Russell v. Choicepoint,* 300 FSupp2d 450, 453 (EDLa 2004), re DPPA: Permissible uses of personal information are listed in 18 U.S.C. § 2721(b). *Baker v. Bronx-Westchester Investigations,* 850 FSupp 260 (SDNY 1994), re FCRA *Trans Union LLC v. F.T.C.,* 295 F3d (DC 2002), re G-L-B-A.

5. *Schulman v. Group W,* 59 CalRptr2d 434, 455 (Cal 1996).

6. *U.S. v. Raines,* 536 F2d 796 (8th Cir 1976).

7. *People v. Segal,* 358 NYS2d 866, 871 (NY 1974).

8. *Harris v. Carbonneau,* 685 A2d 296, 300 (Vt 1996).

9. *Madruga v. County of Riverside,* 431 FSupp2d 1049, 1055 (CDCal 2005).

10. *Mauri v. Smith,* 901 P2d 247, 253 (Or 1995).

11. *State v. Hagwood,* 2005 Ohio 2131 (Oh 2005).

12. *People v. Morgan,* 337 NE2d 400 (Ill 1975).

13. *People v. Segal,* 358 NYS2d 866, 871 (NY 1974).

14. *Keyzer v. Amerlink,* Ltd., 618 SE2d 768, 773 (NC 2005).

15. *Desnick v. ABC,* 44 F3d 1345, 1352 (7th Cir 1995).

16. *Lemon v. State,* 289 SE2d 789 (Ga 1982).

17. *Brown v. State,* 140 So2d 565, 565 (Miss 1962).

18. *Miller v. Brooks,* 472 SE2d 350 (NC 1996).

19. *Miller v. Brooks,* 472 SE2d 350, 354 (NC 1996).

20. *Burns v. Masterbrand Cabinets Inc.,* 874 NE2d 72 (Ill 2007).

21. *Machleder v. Diaz,* 538 FSupp 1364, 1374 (SDNY 1982).

22. *Shulman v. Group W,* 59 CalRptr2d 434, 455 (Cal 1996).

23. *Furman v. Sheppard,* 744 A2d 583 (Md 1998).

24. *Miller v. Brooks,* 472 SE2d 350, 354 (NC 1996).

25. *Furman v. Sheppard,* 744 A2d 583 (Md 1998).

26. *McLain v. Boise Cascade,* 533 P2d 343 (Or 1975).

27. *U.S. v. Taborda,* 635 P2d 131 (2nd Cir 1980).

28. *U.S. v. Taborda,* 635 P2d 131, 138-139 (2nd Cir 1980).

29. *State v. Jackson,* 2002 WA 689 (83) (WACA 2001).

30. *State v. Ludvik,* 698 P2d 1064 (Wash 1985).

31. *Souder v. Pendleton,* 88 So2d 716, 717 (La 1956).

32. *U.S. v. Cuevas,* 821 F2d 248 (5th Cir 1987).

33. *California v. Ciraolo,* 476 U.S. 207, 213 (1986).

34. *U.S. v. Whaley,* 779 P2d 585, 591 (11th Cir 1986).

35. *State v. Louis,* 672 P2d 708 (Or 1983).

36. *State v. Vogel,* 428 NW2d 272 (SD 1988).

37. *U.S. v. Kim,* 415 F.Supp. 1252, 1256 (Haw 1976).

38. *Burns v. Masterbrand Cabinets Inc.,* 874 NE2d 72 (Ill 2007).

39. *Johnson v. K-Mart,* 7232 NE2d 1192 (Ill 2000).

40. *Souder v. Pendleton,* 88 So2d 716, 717 (La 1956).

41. *Pinkerton Nat. Detective Agency v. Stevens,* 132 SE2d 119, 120 (Ga 1963).

42. *Noble v. Sears,* 109 CalRptr 269, 272 (Cal 1973).

{The investigator} contacted an attendant at {his client's spouse's} health club and asked him how long he had been having an affair with her...Those words, portraying {her} as an unfaithful spouse...could amount to actionable defamation unless privileged...The issue before us, then, is whether the {investigator's} statements were... privileged. *Hawkins v. Harris,* 661 A2d 284, 289 (NJ 1995)

5.1 INTRODUCTION

The gumshoe spread half a dozen still photos across the desk in front of his client. The man who had been standing perused them before sinking hard onto a metal stack chair. "Never thought she'd do this to me," he said, shoulders slumped, chin just off the closest glossy. "We've been married a long time." The detective handed him a paper towel and the man wiped his eyes. "A very long time."

The detective nodded he understood, because he did, having heard the same words many times before. The dick sat quietly for another moment, till he could no longer contain himself; then in hushed tones, almost reverently, he said: "If you think the pictures are good—wait till you see the videos!"

The detective is the messenger, the man in black, the bearer of ill-wind. The hapless gumshoe is in the business of communicating bad news—very bad news. One day he will deliver an accusation that crushes the soul: that a twenty-year marriage has crumbled, the next that a trusted employee is stealing from the company, or that a son or daughter is running with a drug crowd. It is lonely work.

He does not have the aura of a priest; instead, he relates what he saw with the bedside manner of Hammer & Spade, LLC, crude, perhaps, and somewhat blunt, but dead-on accurate—and it is the accuracy of the accusation, and how and to whom it is delivered, that concerns us most, since it may well determine the detective's longevity in the business.

> *In Illinois,* a court warned of the risks in using any accusation not checked for accuracy. "One who publishes a false and defamatory communication concerning a private person is subject to liability if he knows that the statement is false and that it defames the other; acts in reckless disregard of these matters, or acts negligently in failing to ascertain them." [1]

When the time comes to tell the client that his wife has been naughty, the detective may not realize he is about to undertake an act more fraught with litigation than even the testy surveillance he undertook to get the information. The two-page report he delivers to document his work is more than a testament to a job well done. It is a permanent record that he is accusing the spouse and her lover of an illicit act. So his accusation better be right, and he better deliver it in the right way, and to the right person.

Private Operatives and Their Reports

The statutory authority of a private operative to protect persons and merchandise, secure evidence, and report on the activities of an individual does not include protection from a claim of false accusation.

> *In New Jersey,* the court brushed aside a detective's claim that he had such protection:
> {The detective} urges...an absolute privilege that {since} he is a private detective, {he is}...thus protected from any claim upon the falsity of his reports. No authority is cited for this proposition. It is inconceivable...the court would find itself pre-

cluded from examining the good faith of {the detective} in submitting his report to {his client}. [2]

The most common reaction of any target when accused of wrongdoing—by no means limited to crooks or cheats—is to claim innocence and that he has been falsely accused. In fact, that's almost the rule after he gets legal advice. Deny, deny, deny. The private eye must be prepared to substantiate his allegations, keeping in mind that defamation may be communicated verbally as well as in writing. [3]

5.2   DEFAMATION

Defamation is a written or verbal accusation which impeaches the integrity or character of a person, resulting in damage to his reputation in the community.

There are *five essential elements* to defamation:

(1) The accusation is false; and
(2) it impeaches the subject's character; and
(3) it is published to a third person; and
(4) it damages the reputation of the subject; and
(5) that the accusation is done intentionally or with fault such as wanton disregard of facts. [4]

The first key is that the accusation be false. "{F}alsity is an essential element to a libel action; therefore, a true statement cannot provide the basis for such action." [5] On the flip side, it is only necessary to prove the communication is substantially true to defeat the claim of defamation; that the "sting" of the accusation may not have been entirely true, but was substantially true. [6]

5.3   TYPES OF DEFAMATION: PER SE AND PER QUOD

Accusations come in two varieties with key differences: defamation per se and defamation per quod. For the private operative, it's time well spent to review the differences.

Defamation Per Se

An accusation is defamatory per se when mere utterance of the words to a third person damages an individual's reputation. Whether spoken or written, the accusation, when revealed to another person, even the individual's spouse, is devastating to his reputation.

There are five accusations which constitute a per se defamation; each represents a common type accusation made by a private operative but which might be better avoided. The five are actionable because the "sting" of the accusation tends to immediately and forevermore identify the subject as a person of poor character who cannot be trusted.

Warning It behooves a private operative to treat the following five accusations like he would a Wisconsin deer hunter standing between him and the tavern door at last call. If there's another way out, use it!

The Five Accusations of Defamation Per Se

(1) The subject has committed a criminal offense; or
(2) has a communicable disease; or
(3) cannot perform his job; or
(4) is unprofessional in his occupation or trade; or
(5) is guilty of adultery and fornication (not actionable in all jurisdictions, but in those in which it applies, it is by far the most problematic for private detectives). [7]

Malice in Law

Malice—bad motive or intention—is assumed in making any of the five accusations. Bad motive is implied since the words are "so obviously and naturally hurtful that proof of injury is not necessary." As a consequence, an individual so defamed has a free ticket to damages—he needs no proof of actual damage to his reputation—which avoids the most troublesome area of proof—not that the words were spoken, but did they injure his reputation. [8]

Defamation Per Quod

The second category of accusation is a slanderous innuendo. A different species this, with proof required the accusation did any damage to reputation; and, if so, in what amount. Such proof is often problematic at best. [9] For example, "Johnny Jones accompanied a woman not his wife to the movie house. From time to time, they were seen to whisper in one another's ear." This innuendo is possibly defamatory per quod, but would require considerable proof to show injury.

Malice in Fact

Actual malice or bad intentions—malice in fact—must be established to prove defamation per quod. This requires a showing of ill-will, evil motive, an intention to injure, or a wanton disregard for correct facts. [10]

5.4	DEFENSES TO DEFAMATION

A detective working his trade has ample opportunity to make inadvertent accusations on a regular basis. He is reassured to know there are viable defenses to any accusation:

Truth

A false accusation is an essential element of defamation; therefore, the converse is equally true: a true statement, regardless of the motive of the detective, is not defamatory. The "defendant may...defeat the claim by showing that the statement, although not technically true in every respect, was substantially true." [11]

Rule of Innocent Construction

The rule of innocent construction puts an innocent spin on words if the innocent meaning fits the context in which the words are used. The innocent construction rule is available to defend against both the per se and per quod accusation. Courts apply the allegedly injurious words to their natural and obvious meaning, but if they are capable of an innocent construction, they are so understood. [12]

The rule requires the innocent meaning not be based on a thin subjective argument. Courts will not strain to find an innocent meaning when the defamatory meaning is the more reasonable.

> *In Ohio,* the phrase "he is a convicted sexual offender" was held not susceptible of any meaning other than imputation of a criminal conviction. [13]

> *In Illinois,* the court ruled that when a defendant called a woman a "slut" he intended the modern meaning of sexual un-chastity, not a one-hundred year-old meaning of a "bold, brazen girl." The utterance was defamation per se and cost the speaker money. [14]

Privilege

There are two privileges available to defend against defamation: absolute and qualified. When available, these privileges protect the operative from liability despite the untruthfulness of an accusation.

Absolute Privilege

In some jurisdictions, the gumshoe is shielded against liability for a defamatory accusation furnished in anticipation of litigation. That is, the detective has civil immunity against lawsuits for statements he provides pursuant to an investigation in preparation for litigation. However, the accusation must be made in anticipation of litigation, not as a result of litigation. Also, the protection is civil only, and does not protect against criminal perjury charges—an accusation made under oath when knowingly false. [15]

In New Jersey, a private detective made up a phony surveillance log including fornication sessions of his client's wife, all to run up his bill. The report was not furnished with litigation in mind, but when the husband saw what his wife was up to, to the detective's horror, the client immediately filed suit against her. Since the fabrication defamed both the wife and the third person, they sued the detective who raised absolute immunity as his defense. He claimed the report was used in litigation and therefore protected. The court agreed that had he been hired with litigation in mind, immunity would apply, but, in this case, litigation was the result of the report, not the other way around. Said the court:

Defendant clearly had a duty to those he observed to report accurately on their activities. He is a {licensed} private detective. When the information gathered by him is of a delicate or sensitive nature, his duty to report that information accurately should extend not only to the person who hired him, but also to the subjects of his surveillance—people whose lives may be materially affected by the accuracy of his reports....The entire tenor of the licensing statute indicates that its aim is to impose a standard of competent professionalism upon licensed private detectives. [16]

Qualified Privilege

The operative's bread and butter defense, however, is the qualified privilege, summarized as follows: "Communications made on a proper occasion, from a proper motive, in a proper manner, and based upon reasonable cause {are} privileged." [17]

A qualified privilege shields the operative from claims of defamation for false or questionable accusations included in an investigative report whether written or verbal. The protection is the operative's main defense against defamatory statements he must make to report what the law authorizes him to do and what he observed. There are five condition precedents to this privilege: if any is missing, the privilege is lost.

Five Elements of Qualified Privilege

(1) The communication is in good faith—good faith is presumed but can be overturned with a showing of malice; and

(2) The communication is to a person who (a) has requested the information, and (b) has a legitimate need for the information—that is, some lawful connection and use for the information, whether it be business or domestic; and

(3) The communication is limited in scope to that which was requested; and

(4) The communication was delivered on a timely basis; and

(5) The communication is delivered in the proper manner—that is, not publicly, but with the confidentiality appropriate to the nature of the information in question: If not to the client solely, then certainly only to those who have a legitimate need to know.

In Florida, a director of a college fired an employee, alleging he was a thief and forger, and disclosed the reasons for the firing to a new hire. The fired employee sued for defamation per se—imputation of criminal offense—and the defendant raised a qualified privilege, claiming a defense when one employee discusses company business with another. The court held the defendant had defamed the plaintiff; that the accusation was not made to a person with a legitimate need to know. [18]

5.5	PRIVILEGES COMPARED

Using a totally fictional name for our example, let us say the gumshoe observes from a distance the client's wife and her fellow co-worker, John B. Quick, in the back seat of Quick's car parked in a remote area. The detective believes they are having sex but has to wonder, maybe, they are just checking one another for warts. Confused, he hesitates reporting what he thinks he sees to his client until he can confer with his counsel. His lawyer tells him it is an involved problem but he will research the matter for $250 an hour and get back to him. The lawyer then spends five minutes in his copy of *Navigating the Legal Minefield of Private Investigations*, personally autographed by the author, to find the answer; and, like the dutiful attorney he is, calls the detective back the next day to report, "I spent most of the day in the library, but rest easy, I got your back covered. I'll send you a written report and my invoice." What the lawyer found:

An absolute privilege could be claimed if the detective was hired pursuant to contemplated litigation to report on the spouse's activities. Not the case here.

Or, the case at hand, the detective could claim a qualified privilege: he was hired to report his client's suspected extra-marital activities, and did so to his client, a person with a bona fide need to know; and did so in a timely and confidential manner.

In Pennsylvania, an insurance company hired an investigative firm to do a background history on a subject claimant whose credibility they questioned. The report when submitted contained details on the subject's criminal background. The subject took exception to dredging up old information and claimed the report damaged his current reputation. He claimed he was defamed. The court agreed the information was derogatory but said the investigator was nonetheless protected. He had achieved qualified immunity by providing information to his client who had a vested interest in the information. The underlying good faith behind the investigation was the insurance company's desire to pay only legitimate claims. Since there was no proof the derogatory information was the result of bad faith or negligence, the investigator was protected. [19]

5.6   LOSING A QUALIFIED PRIVILEGE

Qualified privilege and good faith run together. If good faith is missing, so is qualified privilege. Good faith can be lost in several ways:

Prior Relationship

If a pre-existing acrimonious relationship between the detective and the subject is shown to exist, such ill-will disproves good faith. The detective should avoid an investigation in which he or a member of his staff knows personally the party to be investigated.

Lack of Diligence-Wanton Disregard of Correct Facts

While there is serious division whether simple negligence nullifies good faith, most jurisdictions agree sloppiness amounting to a wanton disregard of correct facts will do so. [20]

In Nebraska, an investigative report stated an insurance applicant was a drunk. When the insurance company denied coverage based on the report, the applicant sued the investigator. The truth was the man drank an occasional beer. The investigator did not bother protecting himself by getting the witness, his source for the information, to sign a written statement. When the witness later denied making the statement, the detective was left holding the proverbial bag. He was sued for defamation and good faith was negated by his lack of diligence. [21]

Negligence

Since communication of an untrue accusation is the engine of any defamation, does it really matter whether the untruth was made through simple negligence or done intentionally? Yes, apparently so. While an intentional falsehood is classic bad faith, usually sufficient to nullify qualified immunity, [22] there is little uniformity when it comes to simple negligence; although there is one investigator who comes close to mounting a majority: the credit and financial reporting company investigator. A report affecting one's credit must be right; and if not right, there is likelihood that if the credit reporting investigator did not go the extra mile to make it right, his qualified privilege will be lost. Accusing a person of felony conviction through simple name mix-up can ruin the victim and the accuser. A wise private operative does not retype information provided by a credit company onto his own letterhead. [23]

Also, under *The Federal Credit Report Act ("FDCA"), 15 U.S.C. 1681,* credit bureaus which provide consumer reports to third persons follow a standard of "reasonableness" highly unforgiving of outdated information. The act brooks little tolerance for mistakes made by any investigator who assembles or evaluates credit information for third persons, particularly where the consumer tried to correct perceived errors. Data providers which provide raw personal data to gumshoes specify the information is not to be construed to be or used as a consumer report. [24]

5.7   A BEAUTIFUL PICTURE

It is never necessary to allege someone was seen "fornicating." A good report will report facts not conclusions, allowing the reader to make his own decision on what was occurring in the back seat of Quick's car. After all, does the client need anybody else's opinion of what was happening to his wife when Mr. Quick undressed her in the backseat of his car parked in a remote field? An artful report will

lead the client to the obvious conclusion without a defamatory allegation. In some cases, admittedly, the detective is
dealing in pornographic details in his written report.

"GUMSHOE" TIP

By the way, did the detective in Quick's case
forget his camera? We started this chapter with a
street-wise detective displaying photos to a client of
the man's wife in action to which the detective added
not one word of description. Perhaps this was no
heartless detective after all, but rather an
experienced sleuth who knew the glossies he
displayed spoke for themselves; and with no verbal or
written accusation—there was no possibility of
defamation—*PROVIDING,* he gave the goods to no one
but his client!

Chapter 5 - Table of Authorities

1.   *Rosner v. Field Enterprises,* 564 NE2d 131, 142 (Ill 1980).

2.   *Devlin v. Greiner,* 371 A2d 380, 395-396 (NJ Super 1977).

3.   *Bryson v. News Amercia Publications, Inc.,* 672 NE2d 1207, 1215 (Ill 1996).

4.   *Roe v. Heap,* 2004 Ohio 2504, Para. 21 (Oh 2004).

5.   *Nat'l Medic v. E.W.Scripps,* 573 NE2d 1148, 1151 (Oh 1989).

6.   *Roe v. Heap,* 2004 Ohio 2504, Para. 22 (Oh 2004).

7.   *Suhadolnick v. City of Springfield,* 540 NE2d 895, 913 (Ill 1989).

8.   *Marczak v. Drexel Nat'l Bank,* 542 NE2d 787 (Ill 1989).

9.   *Whitby v. Associates Discount Corp.,* 207 NE2d 482 (Ill 1965).

10.   *Bloomfield v. Retail Credit Co.,* 302 NE 2d 88, 95 (Ill 1973).

11.   *Global Relief v. N.Y. Times,* 390 F3d 973, 982 (7th Cir 2004).

12.   *Owen v. Carr,* 497 NE2d 1145, 1147 (Ill 1986).

13.   *Roe v. Heap,* 2004 Ohio 2504, Para 45 (Oh 2004).

14.   *Bryson v. News America Publications, Inc.,* 672 NE2d 1207 (Ill 1996).

15.   *State v. Cardenas-Hernandez,* 571 NW2d 406 (Wis 1997).

16.   *Devlin v. Greiner,* 371 A2d 380, 400 (NJ 1977).

17.   *Beckman v. Dunn,* 419 A2d 583, 587 (Pa 1980).

18.   *Axelrod v. Califano,* 357 So2d 1048, 1051 (Fla 1978).

19.   *Chicarella v. Passant,* 494 A2d 1109 (Pa 1985).

20.   *Bloomfield v. Retail Credit Co.,* 302 NE2d 88, 95 (Ill 1973).

21.   *Bartels v. Retail Credit Co.,* 175 NW2d 292 (Neb 1970).

22.   *Morrison v. ABC,* 24 AD2d 284 (NY 1965).

23.   *Baird v. Dun & Bradstreet,* 285 A2d 166, 171 (Pa 1971).

24.   *Soghomanian v. U.S.,* 278 FSupp2d 1151 (ED Cal 2003).

Chapter 6

Power of the Subpoena:
Operative's File During Litigation

{S}urveillance films and {investigative} materials are subject to discovery...where they are intended to be presented at trial...either for substantive, corroborative, or impeachment purposes. Thus, if the materials are only to aid counsel in trying the case, they are "work product," but any "work product" privilege that existed ceases once the materials or testimony are intended for trial use. *5500 North Corp. v. Willis*, 729 So2d 508, 512 (Fl 1999).

6.1   INTRODUCTION

There is no private detective-client privilege as exists for attorneys. In almost all jurisdictions the private operative's file reports, including those to the file which he never intended to see the light of day, are subject to subpoena as part of his client's litigation. It's only a subpoena, you say? All in all, a subpoena can be more inquisitional than a search warrant: a search warrant requires probable cause and specificity; a summons does not. [1]

The reality is that when one of the lawyers in a court case convinces a judge that the detective's file and reports are relevant to the pending matter, there is little to stop the subpoena from going forward—unless his client's lawyer successfully raises a privilege known as the "work product doctrine."

| 6.2 | ATTORNEY-CLIENT PRIVILEGE VIS-Á-VIS THE WORK PRODUCT DOCTRINE |

The attorney-client privilege protects the confidentiality of the attorney and client discussions regarding the case; whereas, the work product doctrine protects the attorney's thoughts and reports ordered for litigation. It is designed to protect his tactical preparation for trial. [2]

The Work Product Doctrine

The federal trial system remains the vanguard of the work product doctrine. In most state jurisdictions, whenever the detective's materials are relevant to the trial at hand, his materials must be produced. [3] Even in jurisdictions where the doctrine still provides some protection, factual materials such as detective reports are produced on a showing of "substantial need" or "undue hardship." [4]

In Illinois, basically anything and everything in the attorney's file and the files of his experts and private investigators is subject to discovery except those documents that specifically contain the attorney's mental impressions and those that reveal the attorney's mental processes in shaping his theory of his client's cause. Basically any investigative materials are on the table for the asking. [5]

"GUMSHOE" TIP

An operative must be on guard when a client straight out of Central Casting sits down and says he "just got himself in a real fix," but that he's innocent, and wants the dick to clear him. Taking the bait and the fee and hearing him out could be interpreted as abetment, resulting in accessory after-the-fact charges. A client with such weight on his shoulders should be sent to a lawyer first, since he has a confidential privilege, which the dick does not. It is the lawyer who can then direct the PI's efforts as part of the defense tactics.

Chapter 6 - Table of Authorities

1. *Warshak v. U.S.,* 490 F3d 455, 462 (6ᵗʰ Cir 2007).
2. *E.I. DuPont v. Forms Pak,* 718 A2d 1129 (Md 1997).
3. *Moak v. Illinois Cent.,* R. Co, 631 So2d 401, 403 (La 1994).
4. *In re Seagate,* 497 F3d 1360 (FedCir 2007).
5. *Consolidated Coal v. Bucyrus-Erie Co.,* 416 NE2d 1090 (Ill 1980).

Listening at the door to conversations in the next room is not a neighborly or nice thing to do. It is not genteel...{But, police} were under no duty to warn the appellants to speak softly, to put them on notice that the officers were both watching and listening...In fact, they did not, with their naked ears, "intrude" upon the appellants at all. If intrusion there was, it was, at times, the other way around, as anyone who has weathered the night in a motel room as the occupants next door partied and argued will bear ready witness. *U.S. vs. Frisch*, 474 F2d 1071, 1076 (9th Cir 1973).

7.1   INTRODUCTION

A private detective is paid not just to watch, but also to listen. Listening sounds easy, doesn't it? Well, it's not. In fact, it's darned difficult—both physically and legally. Nonetheless, a street-wise gumshoe knows a few words on a particular case might tell him more than a frenzied mobile surveillance ever would. He is limited in delving into his subject's thoughts: he doesn't often get close enough to hear what the subject thinks. He knows that up close and personal has rewards, but also dangers. But there are times when nothing else will do.

Our detective has followed his quarry for a week at a hundred an hour plus costs; but his client can well afford it; she's the wife of the president and chief stockholder of one of the largest boat builders on the Kishwaukee River and she thinks her man is cheating. After a week of keeping an eye on her well-heeled spouse, the dick has nothing to report. Then bingo—one day the target meets his female administrative assistant at a supper club. Since they came in separate cars, the encounter seems pure serendipity, but our detective surely knows better. By skullduggery, he gets the table next to theirs, and the pretty young lady with stark black hair down, long, over her shoulders, blue eyes, perfect nose and high heels wastes no time in setting the tone.

"I want Anderson gone!"

"Anderson?"

"He had me order food! I'm no gopher."

He makes a laughing sound: a harmless chuckle.

"What's so damn funny?"

"Nothing, you shouldn't have to put up with that. I'll move him."

"No—I want him gone—gone, not moved!"

"He's been with us a long time...I'll look into it."

Voices drop to a whisper, but our sleuth knows they're not discussing weather. A moment later she's back at him.

"You tell her yet?"

A mumbled, inaudible reply.

"Don't stall me...I want things settled."

"Yeah, yeah, sure, okay, okay."

"And I mean now."

"Okay, okay."

"I'm looking for a house. Right?"

"Yeah, right."

The deal seems closed. The detective looks away but can feel the warmth of her smile.

"Great—let's order, I'm starved."

That's it. But with this snippet, more fees are approved and the investigation heats up. In another week, the detective gets lucky: he catches them performing an act on the front seat of her company Mercedes that was best done in private. Our detective videos the action from an adjoining hill and now has the complete intelligence package: either the company owner goes through with the divorce or faces a huge sexual harassment suit from his employee, or both. Either way, feathers are going to hit the fan.

Months later the detective and his report are in the center of a lawsuit, but the tables have been turned. It is his client who is suing, not her husband; and she sues not just for divorce, but also as stockholder in the company. The court's attention turns to the conversation in the restaurant. On cross-examination, the gumshoe relates how, immediately after leaving the restaurant, he reduced the overheard conversation to writing. But the attorney acts incredulous.

"How could you hear a conversation in the din of a restaurant," the attorney bellows, "...without using an electronic device?"

The detective answers, "I have 20-20 hearing."

The judge laughs and tells counsel to move on. "The detective says he heard them with good ears. What's wrong with that?"

The attorney shrugs that nothing is wrong with it and moves on.

7.2   PUBLIC EAR

The judge was right. There is nothing wrong with it. Federal and state laws universally agree that it is lawful to eavesdrop with the naked ear—hearing naturally without a device—provided the listener is in a place he has a right to be. Like the public eye, the public ear permits our detective to listen to a conversation in a public or semi-public place. That is so because the speaker had no reasonable expectation of privacy for something that could be overheard by someone who can hear it from a lawful vantage point. But what if the subject and his accomplice are in a hotel room plotting some dire deed; can the detective rent the adjoining room and listen with ear against the wall? Yes; the conversation can be overheard by the natural ear from a place the public ear has a right to be: the conversation is not protected. [1]

A material trespass changes the dynamics only if it moves the listener to a place he and other members of the public have no right to be. Like the public eye, a trespass does not make the naked ear eavesdrop a violation of privacy providing it does not intrude into the subject's private place: i.e., a place in which the subject can rightfully claim seclusion such as his dwelling, his home's curtilage, an apartment, or a hotel room (to repeat, there is authority that it is not trespass nor invasion of privacy to listen with the public ear from an adjoining hotel room). He can listen to what occurs in these locations but only if he can do so without crossing the threshold by trespass. Likewise, a banquet hall, members-only club, and the like are frequented by the public eye and ear alike.

"GUMSHOE" TIP

Like the detective in the supper club, it is imperative to reduce any overheard conversation to writing as soon as circumstances permit. There is no hope the words, if important, will have the same credibility in the light of day unless included in a contemporaneous written report. There is no equivalent of the photo for the spoken word when the listener is not party to the conversation. Why don't we just record the conversation? Wouldn't that save everyone a lot of trouble? *Because a recorder is a device and the use of an electronic device may break both federal and state laws, in some cases simultaneously.*

7.3   ILLEGAL EAVESDROPPING

The federal and state governments each has separate laws which define criminal eavesdropping. In general, state laws where they differ from the federal will be more restrictive since federal law permits a state to copy the federal rule or expand its restrictions. The laws run concurrently and it is very possible to violate both simultaneously.

7.4   FEDERAL EAVESDROP-WIRETAP STATUTE

When we listen or record with an electronic device we are in the first instance under the domain of the federal eavesdrop statute, *Title III, The Omnibus Crime Control and Safe Streets Act of 1968, as amended and succeeded by the "ECPA," The Electronic Communications Privacy Act of 1986, Title I, 18 U.S.C. 2510, et seq.* The *ECPA* makes it a crime to listen to a private conversation using any artificial means. A private conversation is any conversation to which the listener is not a party. If the conversation must be artificially enhanced to hear, the intercept is unlawful. The federal statute is similar to that of states which have adopted a one-party rule: if any one party to the conversation consents, the conversation can be listened to electronically and even recorded. This permits use of bugs, body-wires, and phone taps when, and *only* when, one of the parties to the overheard conversation consents to use of the device.

The *ECPA* reads in part: {It is a crime for} any person (to) intentionally intercept any wire, oral, or electronic communication...or to intentionally disclose the contents of an intercepted wire, oral, or electronic communication knowing or having reason to know that the information was obtained through an unlawful interception.

The prohibition is directed at "oral communications," which the statute defines as "any oral communication uttered by a person exhibiting an expectation that such communication is not subject to interception under circumstances justifying such expectation."

7.5 STATE EAVESDROP-WIRETAP LAWS

States enact their own eavesdrop statute providing the provisions are at least as restrictive as federal law. Thus, many states have broadened the protection given conversations, dropping the requirement speakers must have an expectation of privacy in the utterance for it to be protected, eliminating the right to record, and requiring that all parties know of the intercept.

In Illinois, the state *Eavesdropping Statute* prohibits use of a device to hear or record all or any part of a conversation unless with the consent of all the parties to the conversation; and this is so, regardless of whether privacy was or was not expected. Evidence obtained in violation of the statute is not admissible in any civil or criminal trial and subjects the listener to civil and criminal penalties.

> The Illinois statute defines an eavesdropping device as "any device capable of being used to *hear or record* oral conversations whether such conversation is conducted in person, by telephone, or by any other means {thus covering inclusively all forms of telephone taps, bugs, and body wires}; provided, however that this definition shall not include devices used for the restoration of the deaf or hard-of-hearing to normal or partial hearing." (See *720 ILCS 5/14-1 et seq.*)

The same statute defines a conversation as "any oral conversation between two or more persons regardless of whether one or more of the parties intended their communication to be of a private nature under circumstances justifying that expectation." That broad definition covers almost all human verbal communications except a message left on a recording machine, a guy standing on the corner giving a speech to a stray dog, and a Cub fan singing, "Take me out to the ball game."

7.6   ONE-PARTY RULE

Under the federal "one-party consents—all parties consent" rule, adopted by a majority of states, a person may intercept a communication where he is party to the conversation or where a party to the conversation permits him to do so; thus, an electronic bug, telephone tap, body wire, or voice volume enhancement device, or recorder, is lawful if a party to the conversation consents, "unless for the purpose of committing any criminal or tortuous act in violation of the Constitution or laws of the United States or of any state or for the purpose of committing any other injurious act." [2]

7.7   ALL-PARTY RULE

Most states have enacted one-party statutes similar to federal law, but a host of states are more restrictive, requiring consent of all parties to a conversation or the intercept is illegal. All-party states include *California, Connecticut, Delaware, Florida, Illinois, Maryland, Massachusetts, Michigan, Montana, New Hampshire, Pennsylvania,* and *Washington.*

> *In Illinois,* a showing that privacy was not expected does not make legal the use of an eavesdrop device to hear or record a conversation. The Illinois eavesdropping statute provides that "a person commits eavesdropping when he uses an eavesdropping device to hear or record all or any part of any conversation unless he does so with the consent of all the parties to such conversation." (See *720 ILCS 5/14-2)* But recording a voice playback of a prior recording is not unlawful; a recording playback is not a conversation. [3]

7.8   LEGAL OWNER AND EMPLOYER BUGS AND TAPS

Federal and one-party state eavesdrop laws agree that not even the lawful occupant or owner of an apartment or other dwelling or business owner can plant a listening device ("bug") or telephone device ("tap") to secretly listen to or record a private conversation to which he is not part. [4] A private detective has no lawful authority to accept the owner's bogus consent if offered. [5]

Federal Telephone Exception

An employer is permitted to use a commercially available telephone extension phone to listen to conversations of company employees in the ordinary course of business. The conversations may even be recorded. There is implied consent to listen to business calls—at least until the talk turns personal; whereupon the listening device and recorder must be switched off. [6]

7.9   INTER-SPOUSAL EXEMPTION

Federal and state laws are in near agreement that there is no spousal exemption which permits one spouse to eavesdrop on the other.

> *In Indiana,* a husband taped his house phone to catch the wife talking to her lover. When he gave his wife a copy of the tape to show her what trouble she was in, she gave the tape to the federal prosecutor who promptly charged him with three separate violations of federal law: the interception, a disclosure of the intercept, and use of the intercept. [7]

7.10 PERMISSIBLE DEVICES

In almost all jurisdictions:

- A video camera without audio is not regulated by eavesdrop laws providing the device does not record conversations;[8] (See Video, Chapter 8)
- A telephone extension that has not been functionally altered and which has no recorder attached is not considered an eavesdropping device;[9]
- Using one's hand on a telephone mouthpiece to block sound is not functionally altering the extension phone.[10]

Warning

Illegal eavesdropping may occur when a private operative runs his recorder during a witness interview—without consent of the interviewee. This violation can be serious—in some states a felony.

Chapter 7 - Table of Authorities

1. *U.S. v. Mankanki,* 738 F2d 538 (2nd Cir 1984).
2. *State O'Brien,* 774, A2d 89 (R12004).
3. *In re marriage of Almquist,* 704 NE2d 68,70 (Ill 1998).
4. *U.S. v. Pui Kan Lam,* 483 F2d 1202, fn 2 (2nd Cir 1973).
5. *Com v. Parrella,* 610 A2d 1006, 1009, 1110 (1992).
6. *Royal Health v. Jefferson Pilot,* 924 F2d 215 (11th Cir 1991).
7. *Lombardo v. Lombardo,* 192 FSupp2d 885 (NDInd 2002).
8. *U.S.A. v. Jackson,* 213 F3d 1269 (10th Cir 2000).
9. *People v. Giannopoulos,* 314 NE2d 237 (Ill 1974).
10. *People v. Britz,* 541 NE2d 505 (Ill 1989).

Picture Taking: Still Photos and Video Recording

{The defendant} contends that he had a reasonable expectation of privacy against being videotaped in his front yard...We cannot agree...{I}n this case..."the police recorded on tape what was open to the public view... {They} had a right to be where the camera was set up." *State v. Holden,* 964 P2d 318, 321 (Utah 1998).

8.1 INTRODUCTION

Between sets, the chiseled Adonis adds fifty pounds to each end of a bar bell, says he's warmed up and wonders if the skinny guy in jogging pants and street shoes will act as safety on his next power lift. These two are the only customers in a local health club because it's early—the man with large biceps likes to beat the crowd before heading home to watch television the rest of the day. He's not retired. He's disabled. The scrawny guy is there for a different reason. He readily agrees to help out but first adjusts his little brown bag with the hidden camera so the pager lens will get a full view of the weight lifter as he runs through his routine—this to record the date and time the lifter's claim for workmen's compensation disability benefits for an allegedly bad back officially ended.

Most private detectives work alone. The profession is like that. Rarely does a case generate sufficient dollars to permit a two-person crew. Nonetheless, so long as he has his camera, a detective is not alone. His camera is the detective's co-pilot, his back-up, his protector, his witness.

With this little friend he can forego having to make otherwise defamatory accusations; he can let the camera do the talking. With this photographic record he can show, not tell, what he sees. The stakes are high in his occupation—our detective needs no reminder that it is the messenger who hangs first. The camera confirms what the detective would otherwise hesitate to report. Picture taking not only diminishes risk of defamation, it also illustrates there is nothing that brings closure to a marriage like seeing a video or stills of one's spouse up close and intimate with a third person. The detective's report with photos in many cases supports his client's suspicions and removes any lingering doubt whether she should proceed with the divorce.

Like all other aspects of the detective and security fields, picture taking is no different: there are rules that provide a heavy fee for those who abide and a heavy price for those who do not.

8.2   PRIVACY CONSIDERATIONS

Once again worth repeating, private operatives move in a world unfettered by the Fourth Amendment; nonetheless, they are bound by the rule of law which inflicts damages for invasion of personal privacy. Operatives with police connections have even heavier constraints, bound as they are by the Fourth Amendment and liability under federal civil rights laws. So all operatives have to be careful: Fortunately, when it comes to taking pictures, private operatives and private special police are protected by an axiom borrowed from *Katz v. United States*, which applies equally to both: "What a person knowingly exposes to the public, even in his own home or office, is not a subject of {privacy} protection." [1] (See **The Search,** page 132)

8.3	SURVEILLANCE PHOTOS

Photos from the Public-way

It is axiomatic that picture taking from the public street or a position lawfully accessible to the public eye is the definitive vantage point the gumshoe camera-person seeks. However, when the view is enhanced beyond what someone can see with natural eyesight from that location, such as when a private detective trespasses onto private property, whether that of the subject or of another, and takes a picture he could not otherwise get, he enters a danger zone. [2] Thus, using a neighbor's property to snap photos, or using a ladder to look over a fence into a back yard—the fence indicating the owner expected privacy—risks privacy infringement. [3] The trespass is not the crux; it is the enhanced view resulting from the trespass which invades privacy. By the same reasoning, snapping an overhead photo from an airplane is not considered a privacy infringement; the plane is where it should be and the viewer is in a place he has a right to be. The subject should have anticipated he could be seen from the air, a lawful place to be; and the photo is only recording what the viewer's eye can see. [4]

Camera Zoom

Every so often a detective will find himself photographing activity inside a residence or other private property from a public vantage point. This photo-taking is not to peep for any reason other than to ferret out the answer to some puzzle to which the law permits an answer. The view illustrates the principle that what a subject exposes to the public is not worthy of privacy protection. The detective is entitled to record what he can see from the street (or, as indicated, the air). But things grow more complicated when a zoom lens is attached to the camera since a zoom lens enhances the view just like a blatant trespass might. This enhanced zoom view may delve into the depths of the bedroom that could not otherwise be seen with the naked eye from a lawful vantage point and might well catch a court on a bad day (bad, that is, for the detective!).

There is authority, however, that the zoom lens standard with store-bought video presents no privacy issues; that such a camera and lens are not "sophisticated gadgetry" or "special equipment not generally in use." [5] But a zoom lens with the power of a telescope does present serious privacy issues: these devices should not be used for the purpose of making an official record of a privacy invasion, whether the view is by a private operative or private special police. The potential for privacy intrusion is the same. (See **Never Scope a Private Place**, page 49)

Photos by Trespass

A photo taken from a vantage point reached by trespass goes hand in hand with invasion of privacy. We know that trespass and invasion of privacy are separate issues, and that a court can find one without the other. But we also know that trespass onto private property is more apt to invade privacy than a view from a lawful vantage point. A public setting may also provide a reasonable expectation of privacy, such as dressing rooms and toilets, but this expectation is not reasonable when the area is used for unlawful purposes: four shoes with feet in them in a toilet stall being one example. [6]

Warning

We are reminded that a good ruse has its place: that a ruse used to procure consent to enter any public or semi-public area is arguably authority to enter. But a detective must never use a ruse to enter living spaces, restricted or posted areas. These restricted areas include, of course, areas that by custom, usage, and special dangers a detective must avoid. They include locker rooms, toilets, government buildings, hospital rooms, and the like.

8.4   FEDERAL AND STATE LAWS

The federal *Electronic Communications Privacy Act of 1986* does not prohibit photographing or silent video recording—just audio recording under the prescribed circumstances (See **Eavesdropping**, page 75). The fact is the act does not mention video recording at all. "Silent video recordings do not hear sound {and} do not accomplish the 'aural acquisition' of anything." [7]

States have legislative authority to prohibit blanket video recording; but this has not been the general practice. However, there are state statutes separate and apart from the eavesdrop laws that prohibit specific instances of videotaping such as in restrooms and tanning salons. (See sample statute, *Unauthorized Videotaping, Illinois 720 ILCS 5/26-4)*

Warning The audio feature of the video camera must be disabled or the detective may be in violation of the eavesdropping laws of his state—in a two-party state audio recording is unlawful unless approved by all parties involved. In such event it would be unwise for the detective to release a copy of the video with audio even to his client (perhaps, *especially* to his client, who is the one most apt to indiscreetly use the audio notwithstanding a vow of absolute discretion and secrecy!).

Chapter 8 - Table of Authorities

1. *Katz v. United States,* 389 U.S. 347, 351 (1967).

2. *State v. Holden,* 964 P2d 318, 321 (Ut 1998).

3. *U.S. v. Cuevas-Sanchez,* 821 F2d 248 (5th Cir 1987).

4. *California v. Ciraolo,* 476 U.S. 207 (1986).

5. *State v. Vogel,* 428 NW2d 272, 275 (SD 1988).

6. *Johnson v. Allen,* 613 SE2d 657, 660 (Ga 2005).

7. *United States v. Koyomejian,* 970 F 2d 536, 551 (9th Cir 1992).

Use of the GPS device is reasonably viewed as merely sense augmenting, revealing open-view information of what might easily be seen from a lawful vantage point without such aids...The GPS devices made {the defendant's} vehicle visible or identifiable as though the officers had merely cleaned his license plates. *State v. Jackson,* 2002 WA 689 (84) (WACA 2002).

9.1   INTRODUCTION

The gumshoe has tailed the gray Chevrolet for what seems like two hours but by the clock is less than forty minutes. Still, grueling work with a target he knows is using his side-view mirror way too much. The assignment: pick up the subject when he leaves the bar where he is co-owner and find out where he goes. Lately he's been belligerent at work and disappearing for long periods during the day and his business partner, fellow owner of a gay north-side bar, is convinced he's on drugs...again. "Find out what he's up to," says the partner, plunking down enough for the day.

Eventually the trip works its way downtown. At times he thought he was made, so the gumshoe did what he knows usually works to avoid discovery: he let cars come between them, a nervous proposition, but so far so good. The subject seemed oblivious. It's stressful work, but the detective feels lucky, so far no interloper has stopped short at a red light letting the Chevy driver go on his way. It's a long shot to follow someone for that long and not be discovered. About now, the private eye has a warm, fuzzy feeling things will work out okay, but he's stressed, and earning his keep.

The subject's car enters the downtown area and pulls into an enclosed three-story public garage. The gumshoe stops outside but knows he can't wait too long. There are numerous foot exits in the building. He pulls into the darkened building and starts up the ramp, but stops: his car's headlights blanket the Chevrolet blocking his way. What's up?

Just then he spots somebody in the shadows coming at him from behind a pillar—in full attack! Before he can react, his car door is open and he's on the concrete deck looking up—a tire wrench coming down—he blocks the blow with his left arm and fumbles to free his revolver with the other, pointing the piece between the crazed man's eyes so there is no mistake what happens next: the tire iron gets tossed and the subject gallops for his car. He can take his time; there is no way this detective is chasing him.

Another car pulls up the ramp and stops: a horn blows ordering the gumshoe to clear the way. He uses his good arm to tell the driver to wait a minute, really a middle finger pointing straight up, this to emphasize patience: for right now the private eye's thoughts are on other more immediate things—ice for his swollen arm and whether he has to refund the unused retainer.

The private detective does not have the luxury of the six-car moving surveillance, typical of the government and local police. The private eye usually works alone, does not have back-up, or an ability to drop back during a mobile surveillance, or a fresh face to present to the subject for a different look. Any surveillance is tough when alone, but particularly so on a moving surveillance. Our detective thinks maybe it's time to invest in the GPS he passed on last year. Maybe the prices have come down. Maybe he'll check tomorrow.

9.2   TRACKING DEVICES

In a perfect world the detective would attach an electronic tracking device to the subject's car and follow the signal to final destination. Then get his pictures and go home. Both arms intact, gun in his pocket. That's the theory, at least. There are, however, some practical problems that must be considered in using a tracker device. The most obvious, of course, is getting close enough to the subject's car without being seen so he can attach the thing before the surveillance kicks off. Then there is the equally considerable risk that the subject spots the device and rips it loose. Then there is a fair chance the thing doesn't work. Then he has to retrieve it. You get the idea. It's a device that has baggage.

Beeper Vis-à-vis GPS

The most basic tracking device is the beeper, a simple device which emits a signal when kept basically in line of sight. Attached to the subject's car, the signal can be followed for about a mile under the right conditions; this allows the dick the luxury of cars between himself and the subject. Problem is with loss of signal, the surveillance goes cold quickly, and the detective will wish for the good old days. Add to that the fact they fail without warning; and, of course, that they fall off the vehicle onto the street.

The simple beeper tracker is like yesterday's typewriter: useful, but dated. Today, the preferred way to track is by use of a GPS (global position system): a memory tracking unit which utilizes satellites for real time signals enabling the vehicle to leave the area entirely and still be followed to destination. Unlike the beeper, the GPS will permit over the horizon tracking. The device permits its user to grab a cup of coffee while the subject goes on his way and is picked up at destination—with an added bonus: a print-out on where the target stopped en route, for how long, and at what time.

Granted they are expensive, as are the monthly internet fees, but that is not our concern here. Our question: is the contraption legal to attach to the car and follow?

9.3 ATTACHING THE DEVICE

External Attachment

Privacy Issues
Use of a tracker device without lawful authorization can be prohibited by statute, as in California. However, most states and federal circuits permit the attachment so long as it is done from a place where the officer has a right to be on the oft quoted principle that what one exposes to the public is not worthy of privacy protection. And "the device {does} not affect the car's driving qualities...draw power from the car's engine or battery...In short {attaching the device does not affect}...the car in any intelligible sense of the word." [1] However, trespassing onto private property to attach a tracking device may be a precursor to invasion of privacy. (See **Invasion of Privacy**, page 35)

Trespass and Tampering with the Vehicle Itself
Some states protect vehicles from being touched without consent. The operative must be aware of laws in his state designed to protect a vehicle from unauthorized physical trespass or tampering.

TRESPASS LAWS: The usual vehicle trespass law protects the vehicle from unauthorized entry. Since most tracking devices are typically affixed to the outside of the vehicle, this type law should not become a consideration unless the hood is opened, or any plastic part is removed from a bumper or fender to make the attachment.

In *Illinois,* as an example, whoever "knowingly and without lawful authority enters any part of any vehicle, aircraft, watercraft or snowmobile commits a Class A misdemeanor." The operative word "enters" has been interpreted to this point to mean an internal entrée. Attaching a device to the exterior of the vehicle, presumably, would not be covered by this statute. Thus far, no Illinois cases have decided the point. *Criminal Trespass to Vehicles, 720 ILCS 5/21-3.*

TAMPERING: A companion Illinois statute comes closer to home making it a crime for "a person, without authority to do so, to *tamper* with a vehicle or go in it, on it, or work or attempt to work any of its parts..." See *Offenses relating to Motor Vehicles, 625 ILCS 5/4-102.*

The word "tampering" has no uniform meaning. Illinois, for example, does not require intent to damage, so attaching a device to a vehicle may well qualify. Most states grapple with the word "tamper" and consequently there is no uniform application. Some argue it is too vague, that the term conceivably covers any touching of a vehicle; but others hold ground, claiming their judicial officer will know what the word means and when to apply it.

> *In Missouri,* a state court said: "Tampering may be many things. Some may be serious, some clearly not so serious; some major, some minor. Under the present statute whether the act done is tampering is a judicial question." [2]

Taking the court at its word that its state judges will know how and when to apply the word "tampering" is not reassuring to detectives working the field. The fact remains, any time a gumshoe attaches a device to another person's vehicle without consent of someone with authority, there exists potential for a tampering charge. It gives meaning to the old adage, "Do it if you must, but don't get caught."

Internal Attachment

Neither a private operative nor private special police officer can lawfully enter a vehicle to install a device without proper authorization. Clearly, to open the door, hood, trunk, or take parts off the bumper or other exterior parts to install a tracking device would be criminal trespass or tampering for a private operative and a Fourth Amendment violation for police.

But why go inside the car at all? Basically, if the detective can afford the device, a GPS is now sold with magnets advertised strong enough to hold the proverbial 150-pound man safely over a den of lions. But we all know any device can be discovered by a wary subject and tossed in the dumpster; or can break loose and fall to the street when the car hits a famous Chicago pothole.

9.4   CONSENT TO ATTACH A DEVICE

Notwithstanding that in many jurisdictions, no authority is needed to attach a tracker on a vehicle parked in the public-way, there still remains the issue of privacy invasion, trespass and tampering. So it makes sense to always procure consent, which is easy to do if the client is on the title, whether spouse, partner, or co-owner. In some states, consent can even be procured from a lessee or lessor; and the common law extends authority to anyone legally with a key. [3] But caution is always advised and to be safe, the operative should get written authorization from a title-holder; this is particularly so if the surveillance is evidentiary.

9.5   FOLLOWING THE SIGNAL

There is general acceptance that a private operative can follow the tracker signal in the public street. In fact, the consensus is that even police can follow such a signal on the public street clear to destination, but not past the door of a residence or any other area where the subject has a reasonable expectation of privacy (his private space). [4]

In Washington, it was said that "what is voluntarily exposed to the general public and observable without enhancement devices from an unprotected area is not considered part of a person's private affairs." Some such state courts have likened the signal to using binoculars to see into an open field or curtilage—a sense augmentation, not sense enhancement—just as the glass would lawfully show what the naked eye could see if the viewer moved closer. [5]

9.6	ON BALANCE

The tracker is a modern day option for the detective who wants a rest from the myriad of risks entailed in following a subject at close range. Like the use of any device, however, the convenience may be short-lived as equally complex issues quickly become apparent in using the tracker: the detective must affix the device, stay within the law in doing so, trust it does not fall off or get weather damaged, and hope it does not fail to work on a key surveillance. Then, too, he must pick the subject up at destination; and later, in an act that might get him closer to danger than any surveillance ever would, he must walk up to the car and retrieve the unit. All that said, there is no guarantee it will do a better job than just following a set of taillights.

Chapter 9 - Table of Authorities

1. *United States v. Garcia,* 474 F3d 994, 996 (7th Cir 2007).
2. *State v. Hale,* 463 SW2d 869, 872 (Mo 1971).
3. *State v. Cantrell,* 875 P2d 1208 (Wash 1994).
4. *United States v. Karo,* 468 US 705 (1984).
5. *State v. Jackson,* 2002 WA 689 (WACA 2002).

Often the same government officials, who vigorously oppose the admission of exculpatory polygraphs of the accused, find polygraph testing to be reliable enough to use in their own decision-making. Federal and state governments rely upon the results of polygraph examinations for a variety of law enforcement purposes, even in jurisdictions where polygraph evidence is inadmissible. For example, the polygraph is used to determine whether there is probable cause to arrest and whether to prosecute. *Lee v. Martinez,* 2004 NMSC 027 (NM 2004).

10.1 INTRODUCTION

The gumshoe leads his client to the only table in an empty store canteen. The detective is meeting his client for the first time to get a photograph of the man's wife and cash sufficient to fund the start of surveillance. He sits opposite a frazzled sixty-year-old who is on a twenty-minute break from the stock room. The client pushes an envelope over with her photo and cash. The detective picks up the photo and sees a pretty girl about twenty years younger than his client. He leaves the envelope with the dough on the table. Not ready yet to spend the man's money, he asks, "What makes you think she's seeing someone?"

"She told me."

"Did she say who it was?"

"I get the impression there was more than one."

"Was?"

"She said she stopped."

The gumshoe is taken aback: not that she told him she was cheating or that she said there was more than one, but that she had stopped.

"If she said she stopped, why'd you call me?"

"I don't believe her."

The detective glances back at the picture. "I don't blame you."

A few more questions and the detective pins things down: if there is any playing around it is during work hours at the grade school where she works maintenance. There is no pattern whatsoever to any philandering outside the school building and a grade school's walls are sacrosanct; short of an informant on the inside, a detective has little prospect of finding out what is going on in the maintenance room of a schoolhouse. A ruse is out of consideration.

On a chance, the detective asks, "Will she take a polygraph?"

"What will that show?"

"It'll show if she's lying...if she's still cheating."

"Is it legal?"

"Yes, if you're not trying to send her to jail."

The detective was right: the client's situation was ripe for the polygraph: no pattern to the cheating, limited funds, and the only issue, peace of mind. And yes, the test was legal under these circumstances. Since polygraph results are too unscientific for general courtroom acceptance, the test is used only in non-jury civil matters where the parties stipulate to testing, subject to court approval. [1]

10.2 THE "LIE BOX"

True, the polygraph does not fit a whole lot of situations for the private detective. But the polygraph is useful in ferreting out dishonesty where there is no pattern which would permit anything less than an expensive, shotgun type surveillance that is beyond the client's limited means. The polygraph is the gumshoe's tool box equivalent of a ten-dollar claw hammer: rough around the edges, inexpensive, maybe not the best tool for detail work, but used all the time. For a client unable to afford a protracted surveillance, the polygraph might be all he or she needs.

A CIA traitor, Aldrich Ames, sold secrets to the soviets for over a year when he was routinely asked by supervisors to take a polygraph. Authors Weiner, Johnston and Lewis, in their book *Betrayal, the Story of Aldrich Ames* (Random House, 1995) report that Ames contacted his Russian handlers for advice since they were known in the business to be experts on polygraph testing. He got a note back advising that he "get a good night's sleep, and rest, and go into the test rested and relaxed. And be nice to the polygraph operator...." As we know, he passed. Ames has admitted publicly he was a drunk, and drank himself to sleep most nights. We'll never know, but his vodka-induced sleep the night before the test may have had as much to do with his passing the test as any note the Russians passed to him.

Since the prospect of taking the test scared Ames, an espionage specialist, one can imagine what it does to the guy off the street with something to hide. Emotions run high for anyone taking on the infamous "lie-box." Whether spy or a marital cheater, anticipation can be overwhelming when confronted with an impersonal machine that can't be double-talked. As to its accuracy, in the hands of an experienced technician, machine test results will probably tell her whether her man has broken off an affair; and for a lot less than the cost of a typical surveillance. If he passes, however, the test cannot assure her he might not celebrate that very night with a new girlfriend.

10.3 THE MACHINE

The polygraph instrument records physiological responses that grow stronger with deceptive responses. Of course, the machine requires expertise to master and interpret— the answers are a mix of physiological responses to cardiovascular activity, electrical conductance, and respiratory activity.

The test itself consists of a question and answer session in which the examiner generally goes over the questions before the test. Many testers administer an open book exam. He's given the questions yes, but the answers will be his; therein lies the rub—part of the psychological game played. After stirring the subject's stomach and pulse by telling him what's in store for him, he's connected to sensors which transmit response data to a graphed chart. The theory: a deceptive response causes a physiological reaction that the machine will detect and record.

Intimidation Factor

Those who have undergone testing verify the impersonal team of operator and machine are intimidating—enough so that someone going up against the team of machine and operator for the first time feels he has little chance of carrying out a lie. In addition to the psychological trauma that prompts many suspects to confess before even taking the test, detailed studies of the accuracy of the polygraph test indicate the machine is at least better than a guess. [2]

10.4 TESTING IN THE WORK-PLACE

Federal Polygraph Act

In 1988, congress passed *The Employee Polygraph Protection Act ("EPPA"), 29 USC Sect. 2001 (1988), et seq.* In general, the *EPPA* severely restricts use of the polygraph by private employers in the workplace. Other than exempted governmental agencies and certain other sensitive industries, the law prohibits an employer from requiring an employee or applicant for hire take a polygraph; and forbids any adverse action against an employee or applicant who fails or refuses to take the requested polygraph test.

> *EPPA* makes it unlawful for private employers "directly, or indirectly, to require, request, suggest, or cause any employee to take or submit to any lie detector test." It is also unlawful to "discharge, discipline, discriminate against in any manner, or deny employment or promotion to, or threaten to take any such action against" an employee who refuses to

take a lie detector test. An employer is also liable civilly for a violation for such legal or equitable relief as may be appropriate including "employment, reinstatement, promotion, and the payment of lost wages and benefits."

Under *EPPA*, except as otherwise provided, "it shall be unlawful for any employer engaged in or affecting commerce or in the production of goods for commerce...

(1) directly or indirectly, to require, request, suggest, or cause any employee or prospective employee to take or submit to any lie detector test;

(2) to use, accept, refer to, or inquire concerning the results of any lie detector test of any employee or prospective employee;

(3) to discharge, discipline, discriminate against in any manner, or deny employment or promotion to, or threaten to take any such action against

   (A) any employee or prospective employee who refuses, declines, or fails to take or submit to any lie detector test, or

   (B) any employee or prospective employee on the basis of the results of any lie detector test...."

EPPA Exemption: On-going Investigation

The *EPPA* carves out a narrow exemption permitting an employer to request the polygraph exam of an employee suspected of theft, embezzlement, or misappropriation. To use the "on-going investigation" exemption, the employer must ensure certain criteria designed to protect the employee are met or the safe haven is lost and the employer is liable for a violation.

The exemption permits administering a polygraph to an employee if:

1) There is economic loss or injury to the employer's business;
2) The employee has access to the property that is the subject of the investigation;
3) Reasonable suspicion exists that the employee was involved;
4) The employer provides the employee a statement setting forth particulars of the incident; the statement is signed and given the employee; is retained by the employer for three years; and identifies the specific economic loss or injury to the business of the employer, and describes the basis for the employer's reasonable suspicion that the employee was involved in the incident, including verification the employee had access to the property.

 Warning
The economic loss referred to in the exemption is loss to the employer, not fellow employees, customers, or other third persons. Thus, a theft committed by one employee on another would not satisfy the requirement.

In Ohio, the court held that theft from a doctor in a hospital did not justify administering a polygraph to suspected employees since the theft was not an economic loss to the hospital; whereas, when a tenant in an apartment building is a theft victim, a test of the manager of the building is permissible, since, if tenants vacate due to thefts, the owner has suffered or will suffer economic loss. [3]

Employer and Police Joint-effort

It is not a violation of *EPPA* for an employer to cooperate with police; for instance, to give an employee time off to take a polygraph test even on a purported work related theft. [4] However, it becomes a violation when the employer tries to use the results for personnel purposes. [5]

10.5 *EPPA:* Employee Refusal to Cooperate

Under *EPPA*, an employee can refuse to take a polygraph exam even if the test is requested in conjunction with an on-going investigation; this refusal cannot be the reason for subsequent personnel action. And should he take the test, results may not be the sole reason for any action taken against him.

10.6 Security Field Exemption

EPPA permits the testing of private security in the armored car and alarm business; as well as private operatives who protect facilities having significant impact on the health or safety of any state or the national security of the United States. These employees may be tested regularly and personnel actions are exempt from the *EPPA.*

10.7 State Laws

States are required to abide by the rules of *EPPA* unless passing a more restrictive law. Long before the current federal statute basically removed polygraph use from the workplace, many states had already done so.

In Minnesota, in affirming that the machine cannot be used in the work place, the court discussed the state of the polygraph's role at that time in the workplace (1981), and determined, by its count, some fifteen states having already barred use of the polygraph and its less expensive offspring, voice analysis, in employer hiring. (In voice stress analysis, a tape recording of a person's speech is measured for emotional stress; supposedly, variations will correlate to deception.) [6]

105

10.8 **USES OUTSIDE THE WORKPLACE**

The *EPPA* does not regulate use of the polygraph in areas other than the employer-employee relationship; so, the device is commonly used in matters involving questions of marital infidelity, business and social dishonesty, witness credibility, or credential background.

"GUMSHOE" TIP

Polygraph operators always protect themselves by having a written statement signed by the person to be tested that the exam is voluntary and not for employment purposes.

Chapter 10 - Table of Authorities

1. *Lee v. Martinez,* 2004 NMSC 027 (NM 2004).
2. *Lee v. Martinez,* 2004 NMSC 027 (NM 2004).
3. *Lyle v. Mercy Hosp.,* 876 FSupp 157, 161 (SDOhio 1995).
4. *Mennen v. Easter Store,* 951 FSupp 838, 853 (NDIowa 1997).
5. *Mennen v. Easter Store,* 951 FSupp 838, 856 (NDIowa 1997).
6. *State v. Spanhaus,* 309 NW2d 735, 743 (fn 14) (Minn 1981).

Miranda, being a constitutional decision of this Court {the U.S. Supreme Court}, may not be in effect overruled by an Act of Congress...Miranda has become embedded in routine police practice to the point where the warnings have become part of our national culture. *Dickerson v. U.S.*, 530 U.S. 428 (2000).

11.1 INTRODUCTION

A gumshoe thrives on working an old criminal case police have on the back burner. Given modest financial help and his robust imagination, a private detective can do things, go places, and talk to people in a way police can't—unlike a cop, the private sleuth is almost always undercover. By guile and tricks of his craft, ruse and impersonation, many a case is broken, a person found, or a confession obtained. Whether at a bar, golf course, or 30,000 feet in the air, the private eye can fuel a suspect with false information or wine—or both—until he yodels like a Wisconsin deer hunter at breakfast. The police officer is not so blessed: when he sets his sights on a suspect, he is close to, or already under, constraints of the Miranda warning. He cannot wait too long: If he has given the suspect reason to believe he is in custody, and has not given the warning, the officer has a lot a stake: exclusion from court of the suspect's admission; and consequent possible loss of his conviction.

11.2 *MIRANDA V. ARIZONA*

The so-called "Miranda warning" arises from the 1966 case of *Miranda v. Arizona*, 384 U.S. 4356 (1966). It was here the U.S. Supreme Court changed how police talked to custodial suspects in a big way—a very big way! In the case, under heavy police interrogation while in custody, Miranda confessed to robbery and attempted rape. After conviction, he appealed and the case worked its way to the U.S. Supreme Court. Until that time, a defendant had a right to counsel during interrogation but he had no right that he be advised of that right. After debate, Chief Justice Earl Warren, speaking for a divided Court, wrote that due to the inherent coercive nature of his custodial interrogation, and, without having been warned he had a right to the presence of counsel, Miranda's confession was deemed in violation of the Fifth Amendment of the U.S. Constitution and his conviction reversed.

Said Justice Warren:

The person in custody must, prior to interrogation, be clearly informed that he has the right to remain silent, and that anything he says will be used against him in court; he must be clearly informed that he has the right to consult with a lawyer and to have the lawyer with him during interrogation, and that, if he is indigent, a lawyer will be appointed to represent him.

The Fifth Amendment
  Of pertinence to our discussion here, the Fifth Amendment language applicable to police custodial interrogation states: "...nor shall {any person} be compelled in any criminal case to be a witness against himself, nor be deprived of life, liberty, or property, without due process of law."

As a direct result of the *Miranda v. Arizona* decision, a custodial confession is presumed in violation of the Fifth Amendment of the U.S. Constitution unless it can be shown the defendant was warned of certain constitutional rights. That warning is known as the "Miranda Warning" (or sometimes just "Miranda"). [1]

Miranda Warning

To comply with Miranda, a "custodial suspect" must be warned:

(1) That he has a right to remain silent;
(2) that anything he says may be used against him in a court of law;
(3) that he has a right to have an attorney present at questioning; and
(4) that if he wishes an attorney but cannot afford one, an attorney will be provided at public expense. [2]

Justice Warren described what is meant by custodial interrogation:

The prosecution may not use statements...stemming from custodial interrogation...unless it demonstrates the use of procedural safeguards effective to secure the privilege against self-incrimination...By custodial interrogation, we mean questioning initiated by law enforcement officers after a person has been taken into custody or otherwise deprived of his freedom of action in any significant way. [3]

Access to counsel can be waived after the warning if the suspect does so "voluntarily, knowingly, and intelligently." [4] Another exception to the warning is referred to as the "public safety exception," wherein an emergency of great magnitude arises, allowing police, without a Miranda warning, to demand of a suspect, "Where'd you plant the bomb?" The public safety exception is rarely granted. [5]

11.3   PRIVATE OPERATIVE

Is the private detective or security officer required to give the Miranda warning? No—the warning is directed solely at actions of government agents, not private detectives and private security personnel—that is, providing the private operative is not in league with police or other government officials under what is called "nexus." Nexus makes the interrogation a joint effort and makes applicable the Miranda warning. (See **Nexus**, page 123)

In Michigan, the state court clearly reaffirmed the oft-quoted principle: The...{Miranda} rule only applies if governmental involvement can be shown... Statements made to private security guards need not be preceded by Miranda warnings and are admissible into evidence against the defendant. [6]

In Indiana, the court said it this way: {Private} security officers, as private citizens, are not required to give Miranda warnings. [7]

In Nevada, a security operative interrogated a casino cheat until he confessed. The court held Miranda was not necessary since the warning is to prevent "oppressive police tactics"; and the "potentiality for compulsion" found in custodial interrogation initiated by police officers; and is not designed to regulate private security officers. [8]

In Alaska, the court in a shoplifter case said: {The defendant} asks us to apply {Miranda}...standards to questioning by store detectives. The cases which have addressed this issue uniformly reject {the defendant's position}...We are persuaded by these {cases} and hold that store security guards, unless acting as state agents, need not give Miranda warnings before questioning suspects. [9]

Interrogation of Suspects

Coercion

Miranda is inapplicable to private operatives; nonetheless, a private operative may not use physical or mental torture to force a statement from a suspect. These extreme tactics invalidate any statement as "not the product of a rational intellect and a free will...These standards are applicable whether a confession is the product of physical intimidation or psychological pressure...{Thus} any admission or confession {which is} the product of the use or threat of physical violence by a private citizen must be excluded from evidence." [10]

> *In California,* a suspect accompanied by his wife was spotted stealing company property. He and the wife were put in separate rooms and grilled. Finally, in exchange for her release the subject confessed. The court held the brutal interrogation of his wife constituted coercion. [11]

Nexus

When police and private security jointly interrogate a suspect under custodial circumstances, Miranda applies. Any such private operative-police joint effort casts a wide net that engulfs the private detective or security officer making them agents of the state. [12] (See **Nexus**, page 123)

Nexus may also bite when a full-time police officer works security part-time. Some jurisdictions hold that an off-duty police officer working private security is always an agent of the state and must provide a Miranda warning before start of a custodial interrogation. [13]

11.4 CUSTODIAL INTERROGATION

A Miranda warning is not required if the suspect knows he is free to leave the interrogation. But, if facts and circumstances are such he can reasonably make a case he believed he was not free to go, Miranda is triggered. "In custody" does not require he be told he is under arrest. Courts look at the "totality of the circumstances" to

111

determine if there was a restraint of the subject's "freedom of movement of the degree associated with a formal arrest" such as would justify a belief he was in custody. [14]

Typical circumstances which require Miranda include police directing the suspect to an interview room where the door is closed behind him; ordering a suspect into the rear seat of a squad car and locking the door behind him; and nudging the suspect to a store security office where he is questioned by a mix of private security and police. "Whether a defendant was in custody for Miranda purposes depends on 'whether the suspect reasonably supposed his freedom of action was curtailed.' " [15]

But the belief must be reasonable under the circumstances:

> *In California,* a person reported a robbery and killing which he had witnessed. He voluntarily went to the station house to provide more information. There he was told by police his statement would be provided the District Attorney and he was given no Miranda warning before questioning. In a 30-minute interrogation, he admitted he was part of the theft, but denied participating in the homicide. Police took his statement and sent him on his way. About five weeks later he was charged for his role in the robbery. At trial he unsuccessfully moved to suppress his original statement. On appeal, the U.S. Supreme Court agreed that the statement was admissible notwithstanding the absence of a Miranda warning. The Court held the issue is not one solely of questioning in a police station. To trigger Miranda there must be more: the subject must reasonably believe he is in custody; but in this case, he was given no reason to believe he would not be permitted to leave. [16]

Routine Traffic Stop

Roadside questioning of a stopped motorist does not require a Miranda warning. The motorist knows that if he produces his license and registration he can accept his ticket and be on his way.

> In *Berkemer v. McCarty,* the U.S. Supreme Court said the roadside questioning of a motorist detained pursuant to a traffic stop does not constitute "custodial interrogation....Although an ordinary traffic stop curtails {the detainee's} freedom...and imposes some pressures on the detainee to answer questions, such pressures do not sufficiently impair the detainee's exercise of his privilege against self-incrimination to require that he be warned of his constitutional rights. A traffic stop is usually brief, and the motorist expects that, while he may be given a citation, in the end he most likely will be allowed to continue on his way. Moreover, the typical traffic stop is conducted in public, and the atmosphere...is {not} police-dominated." [17]

Terry Stop

Similar to a traffic stop, a Terry stop is brief, non-custodial, and conducted in public—the guilt-free stopped pedestrian knows that if he answers the officer's questions he will soon be on his way. A Miranda warning is not necessary during the stop unless the officer reasonably believes it necessary to physically restrain the individual. In such case, the action may be sufficiently custodial that Miranda becomes necessary before further questioning. [18]

Open-air Questioning

Open-air questioning, like the traffic and Terry stops, generally requires no warning. In contrast to the isolation, a suspect senses when the door to the police interview room is closed behind him. The same questions, when asked outdoors, may be perfectly acceptable without the Miranda warning—unless by words or other police action the suspect is informed he is in custody.

> In *Louisiana,* a game warden questioned a bird hunter in an open field on a nice sunny day. The

113

hunter was suspected of setting a bird feeder against hunting regulations. During the discussion, he admitted his actions and was prosecuted. The court said an open field is hardly the coercive atmosphere requiring a Miranda warning. Police are free to talk to people not under arrest to get information without giving warnings each time. Even when the hunter was told to move to a field house so they could get out of the sun, he was clearly not under arrest. [19]

In New York, a private special police officer spotted a handgun lying on the seat of a vehicle in a hospital parking lot under his charge. He accosted someone standing near the vehicle and, after a brief on-site interrogation, the man admitted the weapon was his. The court held Miranda clearly was not meant "to preclude police from carrying on their traditional investigatory function of investigating crime, including general on-the-scene questioning as to facts surrounding a crime." [20]

Chapter 11 - Table of Authorities

1. *City of Grand Rapids v. Impens,* 327 NW2d2d 278, 280 (Mich 1980).

2. *Miranda v. Arizona,* 384 U.S. 436 (1966).

3. *Miranda v. Arizona,* 384 U.S. 436, 444 (1966).

4. *City of Grand Rapids v. Impens,* 327 NW2d 278, 280 (Mich 1982).

5. *State v. Hendrickson,* 584 NW2d 774 (Minn 1988).

6. *City of Grand Rapids v. Impens,* 327 NW2d 278, 280-282 (Mich 1982).

7. *Owen v. State,* 490 NE2d 1130, 1133 (Ind 1986).

8. *Schaumberg v. State,* 432 P2d 500, 501 (Nev 1967).

9. *Metigoruk v. Municipality of Anchorage,* 655 P2d 1317, 1319 (Alaska 1982).

10. *State v. Reinbold,* 702 SW2d 921, 925 (Mo 1985).

11. *People v. Haydel,* 115 CalRptr 394, 397 (Cal 1974).

12. *Grant v. John Hancock,* 183 FSupp2d 344 (DMass 2002).

13. *Owen v. Indiana,* 490 NE2d 1130, 1133 (Ind 1986).

14. *California v. Beheler,* 463 U.S. 1121, 1123 (1983).

15. *State v. Heritage,* 2002 WA 1897 (WaCa 2002).

16. *California v. Beheler,* 463 U.S. 1121 (1983).

17. *Berkemer v. McCarty,* 468 U.S. 420 (1984).

18. *United States v. Smith,* 3 F3d 1088 (7th Cir 1993).

19. *U.S. v. Sylvester,* 848 F2d 520 (5th Cir 1988).

20. *People v. Elliott,* 501 NYS2d 265, 270 (NYSupp 1986).

Part II

THE AUTHORITY AND LIABILITY OF PRIVATE SPECIAL POLICE

Chapter 12
Lawful Authority

[W]here the security guard has powers akin to [those] of a regular police officer and is appointed by a governmental official, even though employed by a private company, sufficient trappings of state authority have been found to trigger Fourth Amendment restriction. Such is the case with a special police officer...*United States v. Lima,* 424 A2d 113, 117 (DC 1980).

12.1 INTRODUCTION

The private special police officer is not a government police officer but he has police-like authority. He is hybrid—neither police officer nor private operative—a licensed private operative with more police authority than his licensed brethren, the private detective and private security officer—but certainly less than regular police. He is referred to as "private special police." His authority comes to him by state statute, city ordinance, or agreement with agencies which can lawfully delegate such authority, not by his state's detective and security licensing act. [1]

12.2 ROLE OF PRIVATE SPECIAL POLICE

State legislators deem it in the public's interest that the private special police officer has police arrest and search authority. Typically, the private special police officer is assigned investigative and security functions at railroads, hospitals, schools, tunnels, nuclear facilities, courthouses, and a myriad of other public and private strategic institutions. Generally, his venue is the location his employer either owns or has contracted to safeguard. This venue can be as expansive as an entire state railroad network; or as miniscule as a one-room public library. The expanded authority of the private special officer over the private operative, whose authority to arrest and search is no greater than that of a private citizen, has been duly noted by the courts.

In the D.C. Court of Appeals, the court said:
> The courts have distinguished actions of private security guards from those of commissioned or deputized special police officers for good reasons. Although both are privately employed, with a duty to protect the property of their employer, the special police officer or deputized officer is commonly vested by the state with powers beyond that of an ordinary citizen. [2]

In Illinois, the state's highest court made clear the authority of governmental bodies to delegate this quasi-police authority to persons not sworn in as peace officers:

> Defendant argues that since the legislature has established only two classes of individuals for purposes of making an arrest, namely, peace officers and private persons, the city of Chicago is bound by those classifications. {However}, the city has decided to create a third class of individuals, a class between peace officers and private persons in terms of authority. It is clear that the city has the authority and duty to take all reasonable steps to safeguard its citizens and property and enforce its own laws. [3]

Warning The arrest and search role of private special police does not normally include participation in probable cause hearings pursuant to issuance of warrants. The coordination required of prosecutor and law enforcement in seeking a warrant of arrest or search is traditionally, and in some jurisdictions, by statute, left to the domain of regular police. As to execution of the warrants, in Illinois, for example, by statute, arrest warrants are directed to peace officers; but search warrants may be directed to others. (725 ILCS 5/108-7)

12.3 FOURTH AND FIFTH AMENDMENTS

Private special police, because they have police authority, are bound by the Fourth and Fifth Amendments of the U.S. Constitution; thus, like regular police, they must justify a warrantless search with an appropriate exception to the warrant requirement of the Fourth Amendment; and they must render a Miranda warning before commencement of custodial interrogation to comport with the Fifth Amendment. [4]

12.4 BASIS OF AUTHORITY

Private special police derive police-like authority from state statute, city ordinance, or governmental agency with legislative authority to delegate such increased powers. The goal of the extended authority is to release regular police for other duties and to relieve them of responsibility to protect specific property.

Statute

The usual mode by which quasi-police powers are conferred on private special police is by statute. For instance, by statute railroad detectives perform police functions on railroad property statewide. These duties include duties as diverse as issuing traffic citations at crossings to guarding miles of railroad property—often an area larger in acreage than the city it adjoins. [5]

Ordinance

City ordinances are also used to create a category of private special police whose duties and powers mirror those of regular police on specific property. For instance, in Chicago, an ordinance empowers these officers with the "powers of the regular police at the places for which they are ...appointed." [6]

Agreement With Authorized Governmental Agencies

Certain federal and state agencies have authority by appropriate legislation to confer quasi-police authority on private special police for the protection of specific government property and to perform other tasks. However, any effort by an agency or police department without such legislative authority to delegate police authority onto a private operative manages only to confer liability on the operative on the basis of "nexus." [7] (See **Nexus Revisited**, page 123)

12.5   LIABILITY: STATE TORT AND SECTION 1983

For the private special police officer there is more to the story than his right to mimic a police officer. Every employer knows he faces state tort liability for actions of operatives in his employ on the basis of respondeat superior (See **Respondeat Superior**, page 18). However, with the broadened authority of the private special police officer, also comes greatly increased liability under federal "color of law" provisions (see next section).

Color of Law

When private special police perform quasi-police functions, they operate under so-called color of law, as the term is used in *The Federal Civil Rights Act, 42 U.S.C. Sect. 1983* ("Sect. 1983"). The gist of Sect.1983 is that it is unlawful for any person acting as agent of any state to deprive an individual of a right, privilege, or immunity protected by the Constitution or laws of the United States. Violators of Sect. 1983 are liable to the party injured in action at law or in equity. Employers of private special police often learn the hard way that they have this extraordinary liability without benefit of government backing which covers the mistakes of regular police. [8]

Sect. 1983 liability not only jeopardizes private special police but also exposes private operatives to color of law liability when they likewise become agents of the state through a linking process called "nexus" (see next section).

Nexus Revisited

When a private operative enters into agreement with a governmental agency, such as a police department, to assume police functions when such agency has itself no such authority to delegate police authority, the result is a nexus created between the private and regular police exposing the private operative to color of law liability. [9] Typically, the arrangement is verbal and based on past practices and bad habits. To save some work on its part, regular police purportedly delegate police duties to private security but there is no lawful legislative authority to do so. The agreement tries to allow private security to investigate on-site crimes and even to make arrests. The practice exposes the operative, his security firm, and the proprietary owner of the property to potential Sect.1983 liability. [10]

In Minnesota, private security at an open-air rock concert arranged with county police that private security would do a spot search of incoming vehicles, detain those suspected of having drugs, search and detain suspects. Some suspects were left chained to a fence for hours awaiting police arrival for booking. The court held the concert security operators had become agents of the state. [11]

12.6   QUALIFIED IMMUNITY

The Federal Civil Rights Act, 42 U.S.C., Sect. 1983, provides qualified immunity for discretionary acts such as an arrest when made on reasonable belief of probable cause.

In Hawaii, a district court said:

> A law enforcement officer is only entitled to qualified immunity if a reasonable officer would reasonably believe the arresting officer had probable cause to make an arrest... Even if the officers were mistaken in their belief that probable cause to arrest {the defendants} existed, they are nonetheless immune from liability if their mistake was reasonable. [12]

Chapter 12 - Table of Authorities

1. *People v. Perry,* 327 NE2d 167, 173 (Ill 1976).

2. *United States v. Lima,* 424 A2d 113, 119 (DC 1880).

3. *People v. Perry,* 327 NE2d 167, 173 (Ill 1976).

4. *Miranda v. Arizona,* 384 U.S.436 (1966).

5. *United States v. Hoffman,* 498 F2d 879, 881 (7th Cir 1974).

6. *Payton v. Rush-Presbyterian,* 184 F3d 623, 625 (7th Cir 1999).

7. *State v. Buswell,* 449 NW2d 471 (Minn 1989).

8. *El Fundi v. Deroche,* 625 F2d 195, 196 (8th Cir 1980).

9. *Gipson v. Supermarkets General,* 564 FSupp 50, 55 (NJ 1983).

10. *Chapman v. Higbee,* 319 F3d 825 (6th Cir 2003).
    Raines v. Shoney's Inc., 909 FSupp 1070, 1079 (EDTenn 1995). ("{L}iability under section 1983 may not be based on principles of respondeat superior alone.")

11. *State v. Buswell,* 449 NW2d 471 (Minn 1989).

12. *Pouny v. Maui Police,* 127 FSupp2d 1129, 1140-1141 (Haw 2000).

Private Special Police: Arrest Authority

{W}e have focused on the specific powers {which the officer}, in her capacity as an on-duty and duly licensed private security police officer, had at her disposal... Because at least one of these powers, the plenary arrest power, is "traditionally the exclusive prerogative of the state," ...and because it is undisputed that {she} was in fact duly licensed {as a private special police officer}... the district court correctly held that {she} was a state actor as a matter of law. *Romanski v. Detroit Entertainment, LLC.*, 428 F3d 629, 640 (6th Cir 2005).

13.1 INTRODUCTION

Both private special police and regular police can arrest on *probable cause* when an offense has been committed. Their arrest venue is generally defined by a geographic area: in the case of regular police, its municipal, county, or state governmental jurisdiction; and the private special police, a specific parcel of real estate under the ownership or charge of its employer. In some cases, for instance a railroad detective, his venue is the railroad yard and line property, which may well exceed in acreage the city which it adjoins. [1]

The probable cause which justifies an arrest consists of "facts and circumstances within the officer's knowledge of which he has reasonable trustworthy information...sufficient to warrant a prudent man in believing that the {subject} had committed or was committing an offense." [2]

13.2 ARREST AUTHORITY: PRIVATE SPECIAL POLICE

The greatly expanded arrest authority of the private special police over that of the private detective and security officer has been explained in numerous legal decisions.

In a DC Appeals Court decision, the court said:
We start with the proposition that *Lima* {citation omitted} drew a clear distinction between security officers...and {Special Police Officers}. It held that a privately employed security officer with same arrest powers as an ordinary citizen is not vested with any particular state authority even though licensed by the state...Their actions, thus, are those of a private individual and not those of an agent or instrumentality of the state. The court distinguished a licensed security officer from a special police officer who has the same arrest powers within his or her jurisdiction as a regular police officer...A special police officer "shall have the same powers as a law enforcement officer to arrest without warrant for offenses committed within premises to which jurisdiction extends, and may arrest outside the premises on fresh pursuit for offenses committed on the premises. [3]

13.3 LAWFUL FORCE

Anytime an officer restrains the freedom of a citizen—whether by physical restraint or by the simple act of pointing a finger at the ground where he wants the individual to stand—he makes a Fourth Amendment seizure of that person. [4] It is fundamental that for an officer to avoid a charge of excessive force, he "may use only such force as is objectively reasonable under the circumstances." Thus, when the badge will suffice, the baton is excessive. [5]

Deadly Force

Deadly force must always be justified: that the officer only resorted to such extreme measure when death or great bodily harm to himself or another seemed reasonably imminent; or to prevent the escape of a felon who posed a risk of serious harm to the general public.

The U.S. Supreme Court in *Tennessee v. Garner* (1985) tested a Tennessee statute based on the common law rule which allowed police to use "whatever force...{was} necessary to effect the arrest of a fleeing felon." There was no requirement the fleeing felon be a threat to the public. He could be killed. In its decision, the Court had just the right case to test the statute: undisputed facts proved an officer shot and killed an escaping burglar whom the officer knew to be an unarmed youth, to all intents a risk to no one but himself. The Tennessee statute in question followed the common law rule and the shooting was deemed justified. The Court discarded the blank check given police to kill by the statute: the Court ruled that henceforth deadly force, the ultimate seizure, must be subject to the reasonable standard implicit in the Fourth Amendment; that there must be a balancing of the constitutional rights of the escaping felon against the interests of society. Regardless of what a state statute might say a person who presents no immediate threat to the officer or other individuals, whether fleeing a crime scene or not, cannot simply be made a police target. This decision was in no way meant to interfere with police actions in bringing down an individual when the "officer has probable cause to believe that the suspect poses a threat of serious physical harm, either to the officer or to others." [6]

The U.S. Supreme Court followed this decision a few years later with *Graham v. Connor,* further clarifying there are times when deadly force may be used. "...{T}he proper application of this reasonableness standard requires careful attention to the facts and circumstances of each particular case, including the severity of the crime at issue, whether the suspect poses an immediate threat to the safety of the officers and others, and whether he is actively resisting arrest or attempting to evade arrest by flight." [7]

Today a typical statute suggests need for Fourth Amendment reasonableness before an officer uses deadly force against a fleeing suspect.

"{An officer} is justified in using deadly force only when he reasonably believes such force is necessary to prevent death or great bodily harm to himself or... {others}...or when he reasonably believes both that: (1) such force is necessary to prevent...escape; and (2) the person to be arrested has committed or attempted a forcible felony." (See *Illinois 720 ILCS 5/7-5)*

Chapter 13 - Table of Authorities

1. *N&W Ry v. Haun,* 167 Va. 157, 162 (Va 1936).

2. *Brinegar v. U.S.,* 338 U.S. 160, 175 (1948).

3. *Alston v. United States,* 518 A2d 439, (fn 23) (DC 1986).

4. *Green v. State,* 802 A2d 1130, 1141 (Md 2002).

5. *Farrett v. Richardson,* 112 F3d 416, 419 (9th Cir 1997).

6. *Tennessee v. Garner,* 471 U.S.1 (1985).

7. *Graham v. Connor,* 490 U.S. 386, 396 (1989).

Chapter 14

Private Special Police: Search and Seizure

{This U.S. Supreme Court previously} concluded...that all evidence obtained by an unconstitutional search and seizure was inadmissible in a *federal court* regardless of its source. Today we...close the only courtroom door remaining open to {evidence seized in violation of the Fourth Amendment}. We hold that all evidence obtained by searches and seizures in violation of the Constitution is, by that same authority, inadmissible in a *state court*. *Mapp v. Ohio,* 367 U.S. 643, 655 (1961). (Emphasis provided)

14.1 INTRODUCTION

The Fourth Amendment is the watchdog of governmental search and seizure. And this dog bites in any number of ways. Here's two: first, evidence seized by an illegal search and seizure is suppressed from use at trial against the defendant in every court in the country.[1] Secondly, an illegal search carries federal Sect. 1983 liability implications for an employer with private special police authority or who uses private operatives who have nexus with the government. (See **Nexus Revisited**, Page 123)

14.2 THE FOURTH AMENDMENT

The Fourth Amendment provides:

The right of the people to be secure in their persons, houses, papers, and effects, against unreasonable *searches and seizures*, shall not be violated, and no *Warrants* shall issue, but upon *probable cause*, supported by Oath or affirmation, and particularly describing the place to be searched, and the persons or things to be seized. (Emphasis provided)

The Fourth Amendment does not prohibit all warrantless searches—just unreasonable warrantless searches. A warrant is preferred but not required. Over the years, a host of exceptions have evolved which courts use to justify circumstances reasonable and consistent with the spirit of the Amendment. [2]

14.3 THE SEARCH

The authority of an officer to search is framed by *Katz v. United States,* a 1967 U.S. Supreme Court case of monumental search and seizure importance. *Katz* changed Fourth Amendment protections from protecting a place— that is, a government intrusion into a place where the individual might have hidden evidence or contraband—to a protection of the individual's "reasonable expectation of privacy" in the place or thing searched. [3]

Katz changed how courts look at the issue of privacy: no longer was the concern protecting an individual's secrets hidden in his horse stable—a place; instead, the focus was whether his expectation of privacy in the secrets hidden in the stable was reasonable. Since *Katz,* a search is no longer defined by the law of trespass, but rather whether the government or a government agent is intruding into a place where privacy is reasonably expected. To receive this privacy protection, an individual must pass a two-part privacy test: (1) he must display an expectation of privacy; and (2) the expectation must be one society is willing to accept as reasonable. So, "...what a person knowingly exposes to the public, even in his own home or office, is not a subject of Fourth Amendment protection." [4]

14.4 THE SEIZURE

The seizure—an interference with an individual's personal freedom or that of his property—does not share space with a search. An arrest is the ultimate seizure; of course, the subject is in handcuffs.

14.5 PROBABLE CAUSE

The quantum of evidence needed to justify a search warrant or applicable exception is *probable cause*: "Facts and circumstances sufficient to cause a person of reasonable caution to believe that contraband or evidence of criminal activity is located at the place to be searched." On a scale, probable cause is far less proof than reasonable doubt, the standard needed to convict. [5]

> *In Illinois,* a police officer found a man with a youthful male to whom he was not related parked in a van in a secluded area late at night. When the officer flashed his lamp inside the van he spotted a photograph of a nude boy on the dash. He searched the vehicle and found evidence of past crimes sufficient to convict the driver of child molestation. On appeal, the court agreed the officer had probable cause under the automobile exception to believe a search would produce evidence of criminality. [6] (See **Automobile Exception**, page 175)

14.6 THE WARRANT

A warrant hearing before judge or magistrate establishes probable cause and makes the approved search ipso facto reasonable. But the Fourth Amendment does not require a warrant for every search. Courts use the Fourth Amendment as the basis to reject only searches which are deemed unreasonable. Under some circumstances it may be impractical to go before a magistrate to procure a warrant; so courts recognize that an alternative to the hearing may also be reasonable, such as one of the many standard exceptions. [7]

14.7 WARRANT EXCEPTIONS

The myriad of private, governmental, industrial and commercial property protected by private special police is so vast and widespread that the undertaking by necessity includes on the scene search and seizure operations. In most cases, regular police come when called by private special police after the subject has already been placed in custody and searched. Private security system efficiency in protecting the nation's railways, government installations, and other vital properties lies in its lawful field searches while ensuring constitutional safeguards. This is accomplished by approved standard exceptions to the warrant clause. What we consider next are those exceptions usually associated with private special police in performance of quasi-police functions.

Chapter 14 - Table of Authorities

1. *People v. Deitchman,* 695 P2d 1146, 1149 (Colo 1985).

2. *Coolidge v. New Hampshire,* 403 U.S. 443 (1971).

3. *Katz v. United States,* 389 U.S. 347 (1967).

4. *Katz v. United States,* 389 U.S. 347, 351 (1967).

5. *People v. Altman,* 960 P2d 1164, 1167 (Colo 1998).

6. *People v. Taggert,* 599 NE2d 501 (Ill 1992).

7. *Schneckloth v. Bustamonte,* 412 U.S. 218, 219 (1973).

Chapter 15

Warrant Exception No. 1: Consent

It is well settled under the Fourth and Fourteenth Amendments that a search conducted without a warrant issued upon probable cause is "per se unreasonable... subject only to a few specifically established and well-delineated exceptions." *Katz v. United States,* 389 U.S. 347, 357...It is equally well-settled that one of the specifically established exceptions to the requirements of both a warrant and probable cause is a search that is conducted pursuant to consent.
Schneckloth v. Bustamonte, 412 U.S. 218, 219 (1973).

15.1 INTRODUCTION

An officer is never one to let his badge get in the way. When he wants something, he just asks for it. Many an innocent, and guilty alike, has nodded okay to the cop's seemingly benign request the man be allowed to "look things over," only to find his car seats tossed in the street. A nod is assent; saying nothing is nothing. Search by consent is perhaps the most common method police use to search without a warrant. The incentive for the officer to procure consent is obvious: it avoids the delay of getting a warrant, proving the existence of probable cause or having to specify what it is the officer is looking for.

15.2 CONSENT MUST BE VOLUNTARY

A police badge is intimidating to anyone without one. Courts recognize that when confronted by a badge, there is a tendency for an individual to go along with what the officer wearing the badge wants and when he wants it: badge intimidation at that moment in time may exceed the consequences of police discovering hidden contraband. It is the role of the court to level the field somewhat by ensuring badge intimidation does not outweigh free will: that consent to search is in fact voluntarily given. To ensure a fair fight, courts review the circumstances surrounding the request, including the subject's age, maturity, intelligence, and physical condition. [1]

Traffic Stop

In particular, courts are very skeptical when consent is granted by a motorist during a routine traffic stop; and they ask why would a driver agree to a search of his vehicle knowing it contains incriminating evidence when he could refuse the request, take his ticket and be on his way? Such good will stretches credulity: badge intimidation is usually suspected. One court offered a list of factors to be weighed before any court should blindly accept an officer's claim that consent to search a vehicle was voluntarily given during a traffic stop.

- Was the motorist moved from his car to the squad car?
- Was the officer alone or did he call for back-up?
- Did the squad car's Mars light stay on?
- Was it night or in broad daylight?
- Was the location of the stop on a busy street or remote country road?
- Would a reasonable person believe he was free to leave? [2]

Right to Refuse a Search

Notwithstanding the skepticism, the law is clear: an officer is not required to warn a motorist that he can refuse the officer's request to search. And, if approval is voluntarily given, the individual has effectively signed off. [3] While there is a constitutional right to refuse an officer's request to search, there is no requirement the officer give such a warning. However, when given, a warning adds credibility to his claim that consent was voluntary. [4]

15.3 THIRD PERSON CONSENT

A third-person with joint access to the property may permit a police search of property in the absence of the suspect. This is a risk the subject runs when he shares property with partners, relatives, or lovers.

Common Authority

Third persons with shared use of property have what is referred to as common authority. The premise is that lawful joint access is lawful joint control; and that the subject has assumed the risk a fellow-user might permit the common area to be searched. [5] Under this theory, consent to search might be given by a co-tenant, spouse, or relative living in the household; or by someone in lawful possession of personal property. Common authority has limited scope, however, and does not extend to any area(s) where the subject retained exclusive control (as evidenced by withholding a key to a locked area or posting the area off-limits). [6]

Apparent Authority

Officers may also search property based on consent given by someone police have reasonable belief has authority to permit the search even though, in actuality, he does not. [7] For instance, a person in temporary possession of realty or personal property of the subject may, from reasonable appearances, have apparent authority to consent to its search. [8]

In Illinois, the subject's ex-girlfriend opened the front door to the police and invited them in. She did not live with the subject but happened to be present when police arrived. When she opened the door, acting like she owned the place, and readily agreed to the search, they had no cause to question her authority—but were very careful not to wake the subject who slept through the search on the living room couch. The search disclosed illegal drugs and the sleeping ex-boy-friend was awakened, charged and convicted. [9]

 The title holder or manager of real estate does not have apparent authority to consent to a police search of rented property. As an example, **Warning** a landlord cannot consent to a police search of a rented apartment, or a hotel clerk to a rented hotel room, or a business partner to a locked personal office or desk. Even consent to the room is not authority to let police in to search for evidence. [10] And while a relative living in the same residence as the subject has apparent authority to consent to a search of every space in the house which is common, he does not have authority to consent to search of areas not common, such as a locked room to which the relative is not given the key. [11]

Consent by Ruse

In Macon v. Maryland, the U.S. Supreme Court upheld the stellar tradition of a good ruse: in belief a revenue agent was accepting a bribe to fix his taxes, the defendant granted consent for the agent to enter his private office whereupon the agent recorded the bribery effort. [12] In one of many others, an owner of an illegal porno business granted access to an undercover police officer to watch illegal porno movies in a private commercial studio. What the officer viewed resulted in prosecution and conviction of the owner; on appeal, the court deemed the officer's day at the movies a perfect ruse and lawful search. [13]

15.4 SCOPE OF CONSENSUAL SEARCH

Evidence seized during a consensual search may be suppressed from trial if the police search exceeds what the officer could reasonably conclude was included in the consent. For example, consent to specifically look for a table model television set does not permit opening a desk; and consent to look for drugs in a car parked in a garage, does not authorize opening the refrigerator. Contraband seen in plain view under such circumstances may often be seized, since the officer has lawful access to the property, but, if the discovery results from a search which exceeds terms of the permitted search, the item may not be admissible as evidence. [14] (See **Plain View Doctrine**, page 141)

Chapter 15 - Table of Authorities

1. *People v. Kincaid,* 367 NE2d 456, 459 (Ill 1977).

2. *Ferris v. State of Maryland,* 735 A2d 491, 503-504 (Md 1997).

3. *Ohio v. Robinette,* 519 U.S. 33 (1996).

4. *Schneckloth v. Bustamonte,* 412 U.S. 218 (1973).

5. *United States v. Matlock,* 415 U.S. 164 (1974).

6. *McDonald v. U.S.,* 335 U.S. 451 (1948).

7. *Illinois v. Rodriquez,* 497 U.S. 177 (1990).

8. *Frazier v. Cupp,* 394 U.S. 731 (1969).

9. *Illinois v. Rodriquez,* 497 U.S. 177 (1990).

10. *Stoner v. California,* 376 U.S. 483 (1964).

11. *U.S. v. Kinney,* 953 F2d 863 (4th Cir 1992).

12. *Lopez v. U.S.,* 373 U.S. 427 (1963).

13. *Macon v. Maryland,* 472 U.S. 463 (1985).

14. *Florida v. Jimeno,* 500 U.S. 248 (1991).

Chapter 16

Warrant Exception No. 2: The Plain-view Doctrine and Related Issues

One of the fundamental characteristics of the Plain View Doctrine is that it is exclusively a seizure rationale. No searching, no matter how minimal, may be done...The Plain View Doctrine is nonetheless a recognized exception to the warrant requirement, for the obvious reason that the Fourth Amendment prohibits unreasonable seizures as surely as it prohibits unreasonable searches. If, therefore, the police presume to seize property warrantlessly, some justification is required for that seizure to be deemed reasonable. That, in appropriate circumstances, is the office of the Plain View Doctrine. *State v. Jones,* 653 A2d 1040, 1048-1049 (Md 1994)

16.1 INTRODUCTION

It may seem axiomatic that anytime an officer spots evidence of a crime he can just seize it. Isn't that what he's paid for? Perhaps some might be surprised to find that the Fourth Amendment does not always agree. To better understand when an officer can and when he cannot take contraband whenever he sees it, courts separate the plain-view doctrine, in which a seizure of contraband without warrant is permitted, from the very similar plain-view sighting, which permits no such thing.

16.2   PLAIN-VIEW DOCTRINE

The plain-view doctrine permits police to seize evidence of a crime—providing four precedent conditions are met—if any of the requirements is lacking, the item cannot be seized; in which case a warrant or some other exception to the warrant requirement must be provided.

Requirement 1: Lawful Vantage Point

The officer views the item from a place he has a right to be; whether the public street or private property to which he has lawful access. Courts have permitted a "small technical trespass" under some circumstances.

> *In a D.C. Court of Appeals* decision the court reviewed the action of officers who took a couple of "small" steps off the sidewalk of the subject's residence to peek into the basement window of the house. There they made a plain-view sighting of the subject's drug factory in operation. The officers retreated to get a warrant and returned to raid the house. The court said: "{A} mere 'technical trespass'...did not transform an otherwise reasonable investigation into an unreasonable search." [1]

Requirement 2: Criminality Immediately Apparent

The officer immediately recognizes the item as contraband or evidence of crime. This recognition must occur before any seizure. [2]

In Arizona v. Hicks, the U.S. Supreme Court (1987) disallowed an officer's claim he knew that a stereo speaker was stolen simply by looking at it from across the room. The Court determined that was not feasible; that it was not until he raised the speaker to check the serial number on the bottom of the base that he knew for sure. The act of lifting the speaker meant the criminality of the speaker was not immediately apparent to the officer and constituted an illegal search. [3]

On the other hand, in another case, a court determined that a sawed-off shotgun reeks of obvious criminality; has no lawful purpose; and, therefore, its criminality is immediately apparent. [4]

Requirement 3: Lawful Access

The officer's observation point may be lawful even if he cheats a little—that is, makes a small, "technical" trespass to make the observation. But he still cannot make the seizure if he does not have lawful access to reach it. The officer cannot himself break the law by entering property to which he does not have access to make the seizure. Unlike a private detective, he is bound by the Fourth Amendment, which permits no such unreasonable seizure. [5] Under these circumstances, a lawful sighting, but no access, the officer will have to content himself with procuring a warrant based on his plain-view sighting.

Plain-View Sighting

The distinction between a plain-view sighting and the plain-view doctrine is determined by whether the officer has lawful access to make the seizure. Under the plain-view doctrine he does have access and may seize. Under the plain-view sighting, he does not access and must procure a warrant or use some other exception to make the seizure. [6]

Requirement 4: Inadvertence

In a few jurisdictions, an additional element is required: that police discover the item by accident. If in looking for one item of contraband, with lawful access to seize that item, another is discovered, the second seizure is unlawful. Inadvertence is not popular with many jurisdictions and is not the federal rule. [7]

16.3 ENHANCED VIEW

The plain-view doctrine presumes sighting by an officer using natural eyesight. What if he uses scopes—binoculars, telescopes, or zoom lens? There seems uniformity that a scope is acceptable for open field work and whenever it brings the eye to the limit of a place the viewer has a right to be; but it may not be used to peer into an area which cannot be seen by the natural eye from a place it has a right to be. At that point, the scope has taken the eye into an area where the subject has a legitimate expectation of privacy. [8] What the natural eye can see from the street or property line does not include the inner reaches of a house, the curtilage, or other private space where the subject reasonably expects privacy. Those who have used scopes know that a good glass will bring personal postcards on the kitchen bulletin board—several rooms from the outside of the house—in so clearly they can be read. The occupant of the house is prepared to take action to preserve privacy from someone watching from the street, but is not prepared to protect his privacy against telescopes capable of viewing clear to the back wall of the house. [9] (See **Never Scope a Private Place**, page 49)

16.4   USE OF OTHER DEVICES

Flashlight

A flashlight does not make the officer's view unlawful if what he observes is from a place he has a right to be.

> *In Washington,* an officer used the walkway to the front porch of a mobile home, which was his right to do, and looked through a curtainless window, also his right to do; and using a flashlight in the night saw cut marijuana on the table. The occupant was arrested. The view inside the dwelling and use of the flashlight were upheld by the court:
>
>> When the circumstances of a particular case are such that the officer's observation would not have constituted a search had it occurred in daylight, then the fact that the officer used a flashlight at night to pierce nighttime darkness does not transform his observation into a

search...The plain-view rule does not go into hibernation at sunset. [10]

Photo Enlargement

What the natural eye can lawfully see through a camera with standard zoom can be photographically enlarged. [11]

16.5 OTHER SENSES: PLAIN HEARING, SMELL AND TOUCH

An officer has other senses beside sight which can be used under the doctrine: he can hear, smell and touch. The concept is the same, requiring lawful vantage point, immediate recognition; and lawful access.

Plain Hearing

An officer can use his natural hearing to listen from a lawful vantage point. Listening to a criminal plot hatch on the other side of a motel room wall is lawful assuming no holes were cut and natural hearing is used. [12] (See **Public Ear**, page 77)

Plain Smell

An officer's sense of smell can establish criminality sufficient to justify a seizure—provided the officer has experience and/or expertise to accurately identify the incriminating odor; and he has lawful access. While there is no reasonable expectation of privacy when the odor of marijuana can be detected by a police officer, courts are slow to accept smell as probable cause in itself.

> *In Michigan,* a court reviewed an officer's assertion he detected the odor of marijuana as justification for the arrest of a motorist and compared the sense of smell with the greater reliability of other senses. The court held that smell alone did not constitute probable cause:

> {T}here is a difference between the plain view of an object and the plain touch and smell.

With sight, the item to be seized is immediately present and no further searching is required. However, the senses of touch and smell establish the possible presence of contraband, the confirmation of which requires further searching. With the sense of smell, even more caution is required than with the senses of sight and touch. When an officer sees or feels contraband, he knows it is present and he can tell who has possession of that contraband.

The same is not true with the sense of smell. The smell of smoke, whether from tobacco or from marijuana, can linger and can attach to someone coming into a vehicle, regardless of whether that person ever had possession of it, or whether it was smoked in that vehicle. It is precisely for this reason that the Court should be even more cautious when basing probable cause on a smell. By requiring the officer to use smell as one factor in a totality of circumstances, it protects the rights of a defendant against unreasonable searches and seizures. Therefore, on the basis of both federal and state law, officers may not seize a person on the basis of odor alone. [13]

Plain Touch or Feel

Sense of feel may justify a seizure of evidence if the officer has authority to handle the item and can recognize its shape as contraband. [14] But once seized he can open the item only with a warrant or if the contents are a foregone conclusion. [15]

Carry-on Luggage

"A commercial...traveler's expectation of privacy does not extend to the exterior of luggage." [16] A traveler cannot expect the same privacy of his luggage contents when he checks his bag with a common carrier as he would were he to carry the bag with him. The bag will be handled for safety reasons and this presents certain risks: contraband may be recognizable by handlers by the sense of feel or smell and seized. [17]

Canine Sniff

Trained dogs have a keen sense of smell and can discern drugs from innocent objects. A dog, trained and certified, can indicate the presence of a specific contraband; courts almost universally accept the dog's "intelligent" input as a non-search; and use the sniff to help establish probable cause.

In Colorado, a court analyzed the great popularity of the dog sniff and why courts find them a lawful non-search in a public area:

Alaska is the only state court...to hold that a sniff of luggage constitutes a search...{and} federal courts have unanimously agreed that a dog sniff of an inanimate object found in a public place does not constitute a search. [18]

Chapter 16 - Table of Authorities

1. *U.S. v. Johnson,* 561 F2d 832, 841 (DC Cir 1977).

2. *Texas v. Brown,* 460 U.S. 730, 737 (1983).

3. *Arizona v. Hicks,* 480 US 321, 328-329 (1987).

4. *United States v. Truitt,* 521 F2d 1174, 1176-77 (6th Cir 1975).

5. *Com. v. McCree,* 924 A2d 621 (PA 2007).

6. *State v. David,* 501 SE2d 494, 497 (Ga 1998).

7. *Horton v. California,* 496 U.S. 128, 130 (1990).

8. *State v. Jackson,* 2002 WA 689 (WACA 2002).

9. *State v. Ludvik,* 698 P2d 1064 (Wash 1985).

10. *State v. Rose,* 909 P2d 280, 289 (Wa 1996).

11. *Dow Chemical Co. v. United States,* 476 U.S. 227, 244 (1986).

12. *United States v. Mankani,* 738 F2d 538, 543-544 (2d Cir 1984).

13. *People v. Taylor,* 564 NW2d 24, 30 (Mich 1997).

14. *United States v. Williams,* 822 F2d 1174, 1184-1185 (DC 1987).

15. *People v. Jones, 830 NE2d 541, 554* (Ill 2005).

16. *United States. v. Nicholson,* 144 F3d 632, 637 (10th Cir 1998).

17. *State v. Peters,* 941 P2d 228 (Ariz 1997).

18. *People v. Unruh,* 713 P2d 370, 384 (Colo 1986).

Warrant Exception No. 3: Open Fields and Unprotected Areas

{T}he special protection accorded by the Fourth Amendment to the people in their "persons, houses, papers and effects," is not extended to the open fields. The distinction between the latter and the house is as old as the common law. *Hester v. United States,* 265 U.S. 57, 59 (1924).

17.1 INTRODUCTION

The dwelling is the epicenter of protected privacy. But even the dwelling can be observed from the public street and what the naked eye can see from there is not protected. Likewise the curtilage, while protected, is fairly open to public viewing and privacy is adjusted accordingly. [1] From there we enter the so-called "open field," an area outback of the curtilage where crops grow, cows graze, and where sits the old Ford with weeds coming up through the floor boards.

There is no privacy to protect in the open field, and none can reasonably be expected; so even a trespasser warned to stay out may be found using a well-worn path to town. And when he mentions to police he saw marijuana growing in the open field and they come to see, there is no privacy intrusion or Fourth Amendment violation to hinder them. The open field simply is not an area worthy of privacy protection and the police actions are not unlawful. [2]

17.2   THE OPEN FIELD

The open field is open to public view; so courts do not waste precious Fourth Amendment minutes protecting a claimed invasion of privacy for an area used primarily to grow hay, beans, or an occasional crop of cannabis. Thus, there is no Fourth Amendment violation when the intruder happens to be a nosey police officer. [3]

17.3   PUBLIC AND COMMON AREAWAYS

Other than the walkways, and other points of public access, a home owner or tenant has the exclusive enjoyment of his home, his garage, his barn or other buildings, and the area surrounding his home. But the occupant of an apartment, condo, or motel must share corridors, sidewalks, and yards with other occupants. Granted he has standing to protect the apartment unit itself—after all, it is his home—but the surrounding common areaways are shared, and he has no reasonable expectation of privacy in such jointly used areas. These semi-private areas are like an open field, not worthy of Fourth Amendment protection. [4]

Residential Dwelling

There exists an implied invitation for a member of the public or police to use the walkway or driveway leading to the entrance of a home unless the owner or lawful occupant has gated, or otherwise closed off the entrance.

> "{T}he home's front door is open to the public to use...Most homeowners extend an implicit invitation to social and business invitees to walk up to the front door...{unless the homeowner} has taken additional measures to impede or otherwise block access to the front door." [5]

What can be viewed, therefore, from the walkway leading to the home's entrance, during hours one would normally receive social and business invitees—dependent on the season, the neighborhood, and hours of daylight—is a lawful observation unless the owner or lawful occupant has tried to block the entrance way. [6]

However, when a private detective or police officer leaves the sidewalk and walks across the lawn to look into the house, he is trespassing and trespass is an accelerator to invasion of privacy and/or a Fourth Amendment violation. (See **Invasion of Privacy**, page 35)

Apartment Dwelling

Looking into an apartment window from a common area with the naked eye is analogous to looking into the house from a dwelling walkway in the same manner: a lawful plain view sighting resulting in neither an invasion of privacy nor Fourth Amendment violation. [7] (See **Plain-View Sighting**, page 143)

Motel Room

Similarly, the view from a public corridor into a motel room is not a Fourth Amendment violation.

In Alabama, officers looked through the window of a motel room at the Shady Lane Motel to watch a drug deal go down. The court took little time to dispose of the defendant's privacy claims:

Our courts have accorded a high degree of judicial sanctity to people in their homes, however, this security against unreasonable searches of homes should be distinguished from the scope of protection afforded a motel resident...In the present case, the detectives observed appellant while they were standing outside the motel in an area used by guests or persons having business there. As an occupant of the motel, appellant only shared in the property surrounding the motel whereas if he were a homeowner, he would have exclusive enjoyment of his property...The occupants of the motel room had no right to expect any privacy with relation to what they did inside the window as it was within easy view of those utilizing the motel surroundings. It is not unreasonable to hold motel residents to the expectation that persons using the motel area might peer into open windows. Under these circumstances, looking in a window cannot be considered a search. [8]

Business and Industrial

It is long recognized that use of the word "houses" in the Fourth Amendment is not to be taken literally—that the protection of the Amendment may also extend to commercial premises—private offices, desks, etc., with a narrow protection provided for anything that can lock or be otherwise protected from general scrutiny. But, by the same token, commercial property has its own equivalent of an open field.

> *In Illinois,* the court deemed a vacant lot behind an office building the equivalent of an open field and not worthy of Fourth Amendment protection; so when police entered the land without consent and checked serial numbers on abandoned cars the court held the action by police did not constitute a Fourth Amendment violation. [9]
>
> And, while cyclone fences and guard dogs may physically bar public access to open areas around commercial and industrial properties, to view them from an airplane at a lawful altitude is not a Fourth Amendment violation. What the viewer can see from a place he has a right to be—his cockpit seat at a lawful altitude—is not worthy of Fourth Amendment protection. [10]

Public Areas

Public facilities are open to view and do not receive Fourth Amendment protection. [11]

> *In Alaska,* university security officers with quasi-law enforcement authority planted a video camera to record the ticket sale activities of a cheating ticket-

taker. She was caught doing the one-for-the-house, one-for-me gambit. When she got caught and complained her rights were violated, the court held she had no reasonable expectation of privacy in a ticket stall open to public view and public access. [12]

Lobby, Hallway, and Common Storage Area

An area shared with others receives no privacy protection. [13] It is not reasonable to expect privacy in apartment and condominium building hallways, lobbies, staircases, basements, social areas, or any area where the public or fellow-dwellers have access. [14]

Workstation

A private work area set aside exclusively for a particular employee can warrant Fourth Amendment protection. This protection might extend to workstation space, desk, file cabinets, and even furniture. And if the janitor is told by the employee to stay away from the wastebasket, it, too, cannot be searched without a warrant. [15]

Public Restroom

There is a reasonable expectation of privacy in a toilet stall—providing the toilet door closes properly so that the occupant is relatively free from public viewing.

> *In Minnesota,* private store security and a police officer joined efforts to monitor sodomy activity in a popular public restroom. They did their viewing from the good seats in the end-zone, a bend in the ventilator cover in the overhead ceiling. The activity itself involved two stalls, one with a very tiny hole cut between the partition walls. When participants were busted they claimed Fourth Amendment privacy protection in the toilet stalls. The court agreed. The doors to the toilet stalls were closed and the unorthodox ceiling view was unlawful. [16]

On the other hand, when participants do not stay within their own stall, and four shoes with feet in them can publicly be seen under the partition to one stall, probable cause of criminality exists and the occupants have lost any reasonable expectation of privacy. [17]

Store Fitting Room

There is a lesser reasonable expectation of privacy in a typical store fitting room than there is in a public toilet stall. Generally, the dressing room is breezy with a cloth door; and invariably, there is no problem in seeing around, over, or under the partitions. Also, there is always the expectation that another customer may step into the room or otherwise make an innocent observation. Nonetheless, not all expectation of privacy is lost, and customers are entitled to some semblance of privacy when they step into the fitting room. The private operative or private special police officer cannot use an adjoining dressing room to look into the subject's stall on a "hunch" something illegal is going to happen. There must be reasonable grounds—the merchant standard to investigate—to prompt the action. [18] (See **Retail Merchant Security**, page 8)

Chapter 17 - Table of Authorities

1. *Fullbright v. U.S.*, 392 F2d 432 (10th Cir 1968).

2. *Hester v. U.S.*, 265 U.S. 57, 58 (1924).

3. *Oliver v. United States*, 466 U.S. 170, 178 (1984).

4. *Marullo v. United States*, 328 F2d 361, 363 (5th Cir 1964).

5. *Madruga v. County of Riverside,* 431 FSupp2d 1049, 1059-1060 (CD Cal 2005).

6. *State v. Trusiani,* 2004 ME 107 (17) (ME 2004).

7. *People v. Wright*, 242 NE2d 180, 184 (Ill 1968).

8. *Moody v. State*, 295 So2d 272, 273-274 (Ala 1974).

9. *People v. Janis,* 565 NE2d 633, 637 (Ill 1990).

10. *Dow Chemical Co. v. U.S.*, 476 U.S. 227, 252 (1986).

11. *Camera v. Municipal Court of San Francisco*, 387 U.S. 523, 539 (1967).

12. *Cowles v. State of Alaska*, 23 P3d 1168 (Ak 2001).

13. *Donovan v. Lone Star*, 464 U.S. 408, 413 (1984).

14. *Cox v. State*, 286 SE2d 482, 484 (Ga 1981).

15. *Connor v. Ortega*, 480 U.S. 709, 716-717 (1987).

16. *State v. Bryant*, 177 NW2d 800, 804 (Minn 1970).

17. *People v. Morgan*, 558 NE2d 524, 526 (Ill 1990).

18. *State v. McDaniel,* 337 NE2d 173, 176 (Ohio 1975).

"Garbage is garbage." *U.S. v. Redmon,* 138 F3d 1109, 1113 (7th Cir 1998).

18.1 INTRODUCTION

Long shadows in the late afternoon, the gumshoe parked at the end of a rural road, and walked around a chain that blocked the entrance to the remote farmstead. Careful to stay out of mud that centered the road, he walked the edge, counting as he went, holes where trees had been removed. A shed door banged in the heavy wind; startled, the detective touched the revolver inside his belt just to reassure himself. No reason to be concerned, he told himself, the place was probably empty—but he was a long way from help and the tenant had threatened to kill the property owner, the gumshoe's client, if he ever caught him coming around. The dispute was over rent, lots of it; and other things including some thirty thousand dollars worth of tall evergreens that had been taken from the property without permission. The question asked by the landlord's attorney: confirm if the tenant was gone and if so where he and the trees had gone. Police had no interest, calling it civil, which left the gumshoe to fill in the blanks.

He could see from the driveway through open windows the place was vacant; and found the back door of the house unlocked and he opened it; and immediately saw on the porch what he was looking for: an ash can overflowing with empty beer bottles and pizza boxes. No reason to worry about good housekeeping at this point, so the sleuth dumped the entire contents onto the floor of the porch, and got his hands full of used pizza crust finding what he needed: on a wrinkled utility bill, a modest hook-up charge for electric at an address in a city nearly a hundred miles away.

The next morning he drove the hundred miles. There he found the tenant's name on a mailbox and a driveway lined with seventy-six freshly planted ten-foot evergreens. A week later, using a ruse, he got the former tenant to answer the door, whereupon he served the Country Squire greetings from his old landlord in the form of a summons and complaint.

Trash can tell a gumshoe a lot about his subject: not just the shaving cream he uses, how much he drinks, or what Christmas cards he got, and when he tossed them, but also whether a key employee is selling trade secrets or has lied about his drug use. This is not idle curiosity about someone's habits or personal secrets. The private eye's obligation is mandated by statute and is part and parcel of detective work—the oath he took to expose corruption, habits, and personal traits when pertinent to his client's lawful interest; to locate persons, and to do all within his lawful and ethical power to develop pertinent facts of use to the client's cause. And sometimes the most obvious way to start is with the subject's trash—since trash is fair game and the subject can make no claim to that which he has abandoned.

Trash can be equally useful to police and the private security police in their criminal investigations. There is, however, an impediment for police which does not necessarily concern the private detective: namely, the Fourth Amendment. As we know, private detectives are not bound by the Fourth Amendment. As for police, however, a closer analysis is required. It starts with the concept of abandonment: when is trash abandoned?

In Minnesota, a court said:
The significance of abandoned property in the law of search and seizure lies in the maxim that the protection of the Fourth Amendment does not extend to it.

Thus, when one abandons property, he is said to bring his right of privacy to an end, and may not later complain about its subsequent seizure and use in evidence against him {supporting citations omitted}. [1]

18.2 ABANDONMENT: QUESTION OF INTENT

To abandon property is to voluntarily relinquish any future expectation of privacy in the property; or to say it another way, the expectation of privacy in the materials is not reasonable. Courts look to the proverbial totality of the circumstances to determine whether abandonment has occurred. Surrounding circumstances, words spoken, actions taken, all are factors in determining intent to abandon property. In short, if facts and circumstances warrant a reasonable and prudent person to believe that the subject has given up all expectancy of privacy in the object, the object has been abandoned.

In the 5th Circuit, the court had before it a typical abandonment case: two subjects carrying brief cases spotted police and discarded the cases. They were stopped, not because of their actions but rather because one of them matched a description of a wanted fugitive. When questioned about the cases, they denied any knowledge of the cases or their contents. The cases were opened, and one was found to contain a weapon, and the men were arrested. After conviction, they appealed, claiming an illegal search and seizure of the cases. The court upheld the police actions and held the cases had been abandoned:

These officers in no way compelled {the men to set the cases down, walk away, and deny ownership}. Under these circumstances {the defendants} could entertain no reasonable expectation of privacy in them...The legal effect of the abandonment is...to deprive the {defendants} of standing to challenge the subsequent searches. [2]

Whether the court makes its decision based on abandonment of the physical ownership of the item or of a reasonable expectation of privacy in the item, the distinction has no practical significance from the standpoint of contesting the admissibility of the evidence seized.

In Maryland, a court put it this way:
Generally speaking, in Fourth Amendment analysis, the concepts of abandonment and lack of expectation of privacy go hand in hand, as the proverbial two sides of the same coin. Indeed, in Fourth Amendment parlance, the term "abandonment" is often a shorthand reference for the concept of lack of expectation of privacy. [3]

In the aforementioned Maryland case, *Powell v. State,* police watched the suspect, a known drug courier, leave a drug house and set down a paper bag and walk away so he could check to be sure the coast was clear before proceeding. He returned then to retrieve the bag but was arrested before he got to the bag. Here the court held the subject had perhaps not abandoned the bag but certainly had abandoned any expectation of privacy in the contents of the bag when it was set on a public street and he walked away. The court said:
Even if {he had not abandoned the item} as a matter of property law, it does not follow that a property owner necessarily retains a reasonable expectation of privacy in the item...The totality of the circumstances compels the conclusion that {the defendant} did not have a legitimate or reasonable expectation of privacy in the bag at the time it was searched, regardless of any property interest he may have retained. [4]

18.3 POLICE TRASH PULL

Since private eyes are not bound by the Fourth Amendment, their concern in recovering trash is quite simple—don't trespass and don't get shot. Theoretically an individual might claim privacy invasion against a gumshoe for taking his trash, but research indicates this is more theory than actual threat. On the other hand, police, both regular and private special police, operate under much tighter restraints—the Fourth Amendment. Police "trash pulls" have been prolific in terms of court activity; and the cases follow a general pattern: starting with trash moved to the curb for pickup.

In the U.S. Supreme Court case of California v. Greenwood, the Court held that when there is no reasonable expectation of privacy in trash, it is abandoned and the Fourth Amendment no longer provides protection. The trash can is not the subject's personal safe deposit box. In *Greenwood,* the subject placed his trash at the curb for collection in opaque, plastic bags. He presumed the collector would mix his trash (which showed evidence of illegal drug use) with that of others, making it unidentifiable, but police got to it first.

Said the Court:
It is common knowledge that plastic garbage bags left on or at the side of a public street are readily accessible to animals, children, scavengers, snoops, and other members of the public. {When defendant placed his} garbage in an area particularly suited for public inspection and, in a manner of speaking, public consumption, for the express purpose of having strangers take it, {defendant} could have had no reasonable expectation of privacy in the items that {were} discarded. [5]

Getting trash from the curb, however, is not always possible for police. Some collection points are on the property itself. In fact, many trash cans never leave the

161

property, going from garage to driveway and back. Courts have adjusted accordingly. "Courts considering this issue after Greenwood have overwhelmingly held that whether the garbage is located with the home's curtilage is not the determining factor." [6] Society does not accept "as reasonable a claim to an expectation of privacy in trash left for collection in an area accessible to the public."

Once a person places trash where the public can see it and lawfully can get at it, even when it sits on a private driveway, it is accessible to police. So, courts have approved trash pulls from private property where police used any public access-ways such as the driveway or walkway to collect trash visible from the public sidewalk. At that point, "garbage is garbage." [7] The gist is "where...the garbage is readily accessible from the street or other public thoroughfares, an expectation of privacy may be objectively unreasonable because of the common practice of scavengers, snoops or...the public in sorting through garbage...." The garbage at that point has lost privacy and Fourth Amendment protection. [8]

State Laws and City Ordinances

There are still jurisdictions where trash is protected from police. Court cases in *Hawaii, New Jersey, Vermont,* and *Washington* protect trash from police whether at the curb or not. [9]

Also, some city ordinances enter the fray, attempting to decree that no one except authorized trash specialists— licensed garbage men—may remove trash from a private residence. These ordinances do not present privacy issues, but protect trash for sanitary reasons; and while rummaging through trash in these cities may warrant a ticket and fine, there is little likelihood contraband seized during such a "raid" will be suppressed at trial. [10]

Chapter 18 - Table of Authorities

1.   *St. Paul v. Vaughn,* 237 NW2d 365, 370 (Minn 1975).

2.   *United States v. Colbert,* 474 F2d 174, 176 (5th cir 1973).

3.   *Powell v. State,* 776 A2d 700 (Md 2000).

4.   *Powell v. State,* 776 A2d 700 (Md 2000).

5.   *California v. Greenwood,* 486 U.S. 35, 40 (1988).

6.   *Hyde v. State,* No. Cr-04-1390, 43 (Ala 2007).

7.   *U.S. v. Redmon,* 138 F3d 1109, 1113-1114 (7th Cir 1998).

8.   *U.S. v. Hendrick,* 922 F2d 396, 400 (7th Cir 1991).

9.   *State v. Tanaka,* 701 P2d 1274 (Haw 1985).
     State v. Hempele, 576 A2d 793 (NJ 1990).
     State v. Morris, 680 A2d 90 (Vt 1996).
     State v. Boland, 800 P2d 1112 (Wash 1990).

10. *U.S. v. Dzialak,* 441 F2d 212, 215 (2d Cir 1971).

Warrant Exception No. 5: Search Incident to Arrest

{W}e stated that a custodial arrest involves "danger to the officer" because of the extended exposure which follows the taking of the suspect into custody and transporting him to the police station." We recognized that "{t}he danger to the police officer flows from the fact of the arrest, and its attendant proximity, stress, and uncertainty, and not from the grounds for arrest." *Knowles v. Iowa,* 525 U.S. 113 (1998).

19.1 INTRODUCTION

An officer may lawfully search a person he places under arrest. The search is to ensure the officer's safety. The recognized fact is that the arrestee is under such stress when placed under arrest he might do something dangerous to get out of his fix—like pulling a weapon so he can run. The search requires no justification other than the probable cause which justified the arrest in the first instance; however, if probable cause for the arrest was lacking, the search is unlawful. For brevity, this search is commonly referred to simply as "search incident." [1]

19.2 SEARCH CONTEMPORANEOUS WITH THE ARREST

The search incident must be contemporaneous with the arrest, or nearly so, but cannot precede it. The search incident to arrest does not cause the arrest; the arrest causes the search. [2]

19.3 RATIONALE OF THE SEARCH

The search incident is to find weapons and fruits of the crime; however, any evidence or contraband found during the search is admissible. [3]

19.4 SEARCH BASED ON ARREST AND CUSTODY

A search incident is contingent on a custodial arrest. A non-custodial arrest such as a routine traffic stop does not justify a search for weapons or evidence. The subject of a non-custodial arrest is not considered as apt to pull a weapon. [4]

19.5 THE SEARCH AREA: SUBJECT'S IMMEDIATE CONTROL

A search incident permits search of the arrestee and the area within his "immediate control." This area includes at least his wallet, briefcase, and packages within his grasp, but, on some case authority, may be expanded to include the entire room in which the arrest occurs. [5]

In Illinois, a sample statute states that an officer may "reasonably search the person arrested and the area within such person's immediate presence for the purpose of:

(a) Protecting the officer from attack; or
(b) Preventing the person from escaping; or
(c) Discovering the fruits of the crime; or
(d) Discovering any instruments, articles, or things which may have been used in the commission of, or which may constitute evidence of an offense."
(See Illinois *725 ILCS 5/108-1*)

The sample statute permits the search to include evidence of *any* crime, not necessarily just the crime for which the subject was arrested; this is consistent with case law.

19.6 PROTECTIVE SWEEP

When an officer is in the subject's home or other "turf" and reasonably feels he is in danger, whether there to make an arrest or for any other lawful purpose, the area may be "swept" to find accomplices or weapons. The sweep must be based on "reasonable, articulable suspicion." Contraband or evidence seen in plain view during the sweep may be seized and used as evidence. [6]

> *In the 5th Circuit,* the court described the sweep in detail:
> First...the protective sweep may extend to areas ...where the police otherwise {i.e., apart from the protective sweep doctrine} then have no right to go, nevertheless when undertaken from within the home, the police must not have entered {or remained in} the home illegally and their presence within it must be for a legitimate law enforcement purpose. Further, the protective sweep must be supported "by a reasonable, articulable suspicion...that the area to be swept harbors an individual posing a danger to" those on the scene. Next, the legitimate protective sweep may not be "a full search" but may be no more than "a cursory inspection of those spaces where a person may be found."
> Finally, the sweep is subject to two time limitations. First, it may "last no longer than is necessary to dispel the reasonable suspicion of danger"; and, second, it may last no longer than the police are justified in remaining on the premises..."and in any event no longer than it takes to complete the arrest and depart the premises...." [7]

Search Incident Vehicle Search

A search incident to arrest includes the entire passenger compartment of the vehicle in which the subject is arrested including secret compartments, ashtrays, locked glove-box and loose passenger belongings—even when he is moved outside the vehicle. A trunk is not accessible to the arrestee and is not searched without additional probable cause. [8]

However, when the arrest occurs outside the vehicle, there is considerable argument the vehicle is not within the arrestee's immediate control and may not be searched. [9] This issue can be argued either way, but at the minimum, most agree, that when the officer has reasonable suspicion the vehicle is "hot"—that is, contains a weapon—it may be given a "Terry frisk."

Vehicle Terry Frisk

When an officer has reasonable suspicion based on specific and articulable facts that a vehicle—any vehicle—contains weapons, he may give the vehicle a cursory Terry frisk. This can occur when a subject is arrested outside his vehicle or it can be an associate's vehicle. Since the frisk is not a search, it does not include closed packages, containers, or trunk. [10] (See **Frisk of Vehicle During a Traffic Stop**, page 184)

Chapter 19 - Table of Authorities

1. *U.S. v. Robinson,* 414 U.S. 218 (1973).

2. *Sibron v. New York,* 392 U.S. 40, 63 (1968).

3. *U.S. v. Robinson,* 414 U.S. 218 (1973).

4. *Knowles v. Iowa,* 525 U.S. 113 (1998).

5. *Chimel v. California,* 395 U. S. 752, 763 (1969).

6. *Johnson v. State,* 226 SW3d 439 (Tex 2007).

7. *U.S. v. Gould,* 364 F3d 578, 586 (5th Cir 2004).

8. *U.S. v. Infante-Ruiz,* 13 F3d 498 (1st Cir 1994).

9. *State v. Pallone,* 613 NW2d 568 (Wis 2000).

10. *Michigan v. Long,* 463 U.S. 1032, 1049 (1983).

Warrant Exception No. 6: Exigent Circumstances

It is a "basic principle of Fourth Amendment law" that searches and seizures inside a home without a warrant are presumptively unreasonable...The presumption of unreasonableness can be overcome, however, when the police confront an exigent circumstance like a fleeing felon...In these situations, the exigent circumstance relieves the police of the obligation of obtaining a warrant...The exigent circumstance does not, however, relieve the police of the need to have probable cause for the search. *USA v. Johnson*, 207 F3d 538, 552 (9th Cir 2000).

20.1 INTRODUCTION

W arrantless searches are presumed by the courts to be unreasonable: "Nowhere is the principle more zealously guarded than in a person's home...The Supreme Court has interpreted the Fourth Amendment as drawing a firm line at the entrance to the house...where even an officer who barely cracks open the front door and sees nothing is deemed to have violated the venerable protections" unless he has a warrant.[1] An officer is taught he cannot force his way into a residence without a warrant; and even then, the law requires he knock first and announce who he is and what he wants— or, in limited circumstances, enter by ruse to save bloodshed[2]—or by exigent circumstances. The ruse is discussed elsewhere (See **Ruse**, Page 25). As to exigent circumstances, there are four, each of which requires its own version of probable cause.

20.2 EXIGENT CIRCUMSTANCE NO. 1: IMMINENT DESTRUCTION OF EVIDENCE

When an officer has probable cause that evidence is in jeopardy of destruction, he may take reasonable actions including entering a residence.

In the 3rd Circuit, the court said:
When {there is} probable cause to believe contraband is present and, in addition, based on the surrounding circumstances or the information at hand, {police} reasonably conclude that the evidence will be destroyed or removed before they can secure a search warrant, a warrantless search is justified... Circumstances which have seemed relevant to courts include (1) the degree of urgency involved and the amount of time necessary to obtain a warrant...reasonable belief that the contraband is about to be removed...the possibility of danger to police officers guarding the site of the contraband while a search warrant is sought...information indicating the possessors of the contraband are aware that the police are on their trail...and the ready destructibility of the contraband. [3]

20.3 EXIGENT CIRCUMSTANCE NO. 2: HOT PURSUIT OF A FLEEING FELON

On probable cause a dangerous felon is on the loose, an officer may take reasonable actions to apprehend him including entering private property.

In the 6th Circuit, police chased a felon through a residential neighborhood. They lost him but believed he was heading for his mother's home. They cut across an open field and in the process, came upon a marijuana crop. Their attention now shifted to the owner of the marijuana crop. When they found the owner they arrested him. At trial, the subject argued they had trespassed onto his property; therefore, the seizure was unlawful. Not so, said the court; putting aside for the moment the case could have been decided on the fact the crop was in an open field. But the result was the same. The court said chasing a fleeing felon was an exigent circumstance; and probable cause that he would be found at his mother's place justified the route taken. [4]

20.4 EXIGENT CIRCUMSTANCE NO. 3: PREVENTION OF HARM

On probable cause that death or serious injury is about to occur, police may take reasonable action to stop the danger. This exception has been extended to the protection of a crime scene. Although crime scene protection as a specific warrant exception was rejected by the U.S. Supreme Court in the 1978 case of *Mincey v. Arizona*, 437 U.S. 385, that case involved a search which extended over four days. Courts have since found no difficulty distinguishing *Mincey* from cases involving crime scene protection as an exigent circumstance.

In Texas, police responded to a burglary call, entered premises and conducted a plain-view search for evidence. The court upheld the search:

We hold that the rejection of the crime scene exception does not affect the authority of the police to enter private premises when the police reasonably believe that a crime is taking place or has just taken place, for the limited purposes of rendering aid to possible victim of the crime or seeking to apprehend the perpetrators or taking any necessary steps to secure the premises. [5]

| 20.5 | EXIGENT CIRCUMSTANCES NO. 4: THE AUTOMOBILE EXCEPTION |

On probable cause a vehicle contains evidence of criminality or contraband, and the officer has to act fast or the vehicle may flee his jurisdiction, he may search the vehicle. This exigent circumstance is referred to as the "automobile exception." The action is so common it requires separate analysis. (See **Automobile Exception**, page 175)

Chapter 20 - Table of Authorities

1. *Brigham v. Stuart,* 122 P3d 506, 511 (Utah, 2005).

2. *State v. Elenski,* 993 P2d 1192 (Haw, 2000).

3. *U.S. v. Rubin,* 474 F2d 262, 268 (3d Cir 1973).

4. *U.S. v. Johnson,* 207 F3d 538, 545-549 (6th Cir 2000).

5. *State v. Faretra,* 750 A2d 166 (NJ 2000).

Chapter 21

Warrant Exception No. 7:
The Automobile Exception

{T}he Fourth Amendment has been construed, practically since the beginning of government, as recognizing a necessary difference between a store, dwelling house or other structure in respect of which a proper official warrant may readily be obtained, and a search of a ship, motor boat, wagon or automobile, for contraband goods, where it is not practicable to secure a warrant because the vehicle can be quickly moved out of the locality or jurisdiction in which the warrant must be sought. *Carroll v. United States*, 267 U.S. 132, 153 (1925).

21.1 INTRODUCTION

When an officer has probable cause to believe that a vehicle holds contraband or evidence of crime, he may search the vehicle. [1] The search, known as the automobile exception, is of the vehicle, not the driver or other occupants. [2]

21.2 AUTO EXCEPTION INCLUDES ALL VEHICLES

Any vehicle is subject to a police search if there is probable cause it contains evidence or contraband—except a motor home used as a residence when parked on private property. Then, like a home, a warrant is required to enter the motor home unless some other exception is applicable. [3]

175

21.3 VEHICLE ON PRIVATE PROPERTY

Some few jurisdictions do not permit an automobile exception search of vehicles parked on private property; instead, police must obtain a warrant or use some other exception. [4]

21.4 JUSTIFICATION: MOBILITY AND LESS PRIVACY

The automobile search is justified to stop the vehicle leaving the jurisdiction with evidence. Another justification used by the courts is that what occurs inside a vehicle is too public to claim an expectation of privacy. [5]

In *Wisconsin,* the court said:
Warrantless searches of homes are presumptively unreasonable, searches of vehicles are not...Vehicles, unlike homes, are not devices for storing personal effects, and they move about the roadways with their occupants in full view. [6]

Probable Cause

In a search under the automobile exception, probable cause is needed or the search is unlawful. Probable cause in this context requires "facts {which} warrant a {person} of reasonable caution in the belief that certain items {which} may be contraband or useful as evidence of crime {will be found in the vehicle}." When the officer has probable cause he is permitted to search the entire vehicle, including the locked center console, glove box, trunk, and any containers—with the proviso that the evidence or contraband sought will fit in the place looked. [7]

21.5 SCOPE OF SEARCH

Scope of the automobile search varies, depending on size and shape of the object being sought: for instance, a handgun will entail a more detailed search than a rifle. [8] In a search for drugs, a federal court affirmed a search of the entire vehicle: "If an officer has probable cause to believe there is contraband somewhere in the car, but he does not know exactly where, he may search the entire car as well as any containers found therein."[9] If a specific item is looked for, then the search is stopped when the item is found, subject to what else might be in plain view.

In Oklahoma, an officer making a routine traffic stop smelled beer in the car. When he spotted a six-pack with one can missing from its slot in the package, he searched the entire car looking for the missing beer can. The court upheld the search which broadened when the officer sighted a marijuana pipe in plain view while looking for the beer can. He now had justification to find the drugs for the pipe and this resulted in a search of the entire vehicle.[10]

Search of Passenger's Belongings
Passenger belongings in the vehicle are subject to search if probable cause leads there.

In Wyoming v. Houghton, the U.S. Supreme Court upheld a detailed search of passenger belongings. The defendant was a passenger in a car stopped for speeding. When the arresting officer noticed a syringe protruding from the driver's pocket, he asked him about it. Honest to a fault, the driver admitted it was for doing drugs. The officer politely thanked him for the information and ordered him and the passengers out of the car so it could be searched. The defendant, a passenger, got out but left behind a closed container. The officer searched the container, found illegal drugs, and arrested her. The Court upheld her conviction: the scope of a search under the automobile exception is as broad as the item looked for. The officer was looking for drugs and any closed container in the vehicle was subject to search.[11]

Search of Occupants

However, the right to search personal belongings does not mean the occupants of the vehicle are themselves subject to automatic search. Unless and until the driver or a passenger is under arrest he cannot be searched. The automobile exception does not permit a person search of any occupant of the vehicle. There is a heightened privacy protection of the person that does not exist in the contents of a vehicle. [12] However, when the officer has reasonable suspicion any occupant of a stopped vehicle is armed and dangerous, the person may be frisked. (See **Terry Frisk**, Page 190)

Search of Containers

The automobile exception permits opening *any* container in the vehicle when probable cause leads there. [13]

Search of Exterior of Vehicle

Generally, the exterior of a vehicle carries no privacy expectations and can be lawfully viewed. However, opening the hood requires a warrant or probable cause. [14]

Chapter 21 - Table of Authorities

1.   *Pennsylvania v. Labron,* 518 U.S 938, 940 (1996).

2.   *Carroll v. United States,* 267 U. S. 132, 162 (1925).

3.   *California v. Carney* 471 U. S. 386, 391-393 (1985).

4.   *Harris v. State,* 948 So2d 583 (Al 2006).

5.   *South Dakota v. Opperman,* 428 U.S. 364, 367 (1996).

6.   *State v. Pollone,* 613 NW2d 568 (Para. 59-60) (Wis 2000).

7.   *Gomez v. State,* 168 P3d 1139 (Ok 2007).

8.   *California v. Acevedo,* 500 U.S. 565 (1991).

9.   *Gomez v. State,* 168 P3d 1139 (Ok 2007).

10. *Gomez v. State,* 168 P3d 1139, 1143 (Ok 2007).

11. *Wyoming v. Houghton,* 526 U.S. 295 (1999).

12. *United States v. Di Re,* 332 U. S. 581 (1948).

13. *California v. Acevedo,* 500 U.S. 565 (1991).

14. *State v. Moore,* 659 P2d 70 (Haw 1983).

{T}here must be a narrowly drawn authority to permit a reasonable search for weapons for protection of the police officer, where he has reason to believe he is dealing with an armed and dangerous individual, regardless of whether he has probable cause to arrest the individual for a crime. *Terry v. Ohio,* 392 U.S.1, 27 (1968).

22.1 INTRODUCTION

In *Terry v. Ohio,* citation above, the U.S. Supreme Court expanded an officer's authority to stop and detain an individual he suspected of criminality. Before *Terry,* unless he had probable cause, the officer risked false arrest were he to physically stop an individual who tried to leave the scene when asked questions designed to resolve the officer's suspicions. After *Terry,* an individual walking away would risk physical seizure until the officer resolved his "reasonable suspicion." The officer's authority to stop and detain is known as the "Terry stop."[1]

22.2 REASONABLE SUSPICION

The Terry stop is not an arrest; although, the individual is clearly detained. The action is a temporary seizure of the individual; lasting only long enough for the officer to resolve his reasonable suspicion, a quantum of evidence somewhere between probable cause, the standard to arrest, and a gambler's hunch, the standard used to place a two-buck bet at the track.[2] If the officer does not have reasonable suspicion when he makes the stop, any action which follows is illegal.

In the 7ᵗʰ Circuit, the court said:

There is no bright-line test for distinguishing between a lawful Terry stop and an illegal arrest...
Instead, in evaluating the reasonableness of an
investigative stop, we examine first whether the
officer's action was justified at its inception and
second, whether it was reasonable in scope to the
circumstances which justified the interference in the
first place...Clearly the thought of allowing police
officers to handcuff persons when probable cause to
arrest is lacking is a troubling one. Nevertheless, we
are unwilling to hold, under Terry, the placing of a
suspect in handcuffs without probable cause to
arrest is always unlawful. If, in a rare case, "common
sense and human experience" convince us that the
officer believed reasonably that an investigative stop
could be effectuated safely only in this manner, "we
will not substitute our judgment for that of the
officers...." [3]

Force During a Terry Stop

Can police use handcuffs or draw a weapon during a
Terry stop? Yes, if they can justify the action by facts at the
moment of the stop—facts they develop after the stop
cannot be used to justify either the stop or the force used. [4]
When force used is inappropriate to a Terry stop, the
seizure becomes an arrest; and, lacking probable cause,
the arrest is unlawful.

In Texas, a district court had before it a case
which examined typical limits of force permitted in a
Terry stop. Acting solely on a tip and the fact a corn
silo was air-conditioned, county and federal agents
jumped a pair of individuals they believed to be
working a drug operation out of the silo. Before the
reasonable suspicion inquiry even began, officers
had the men in handcuffs and at gun point. The silo
had in fact been used for what was suspected, and
the men were subsequently convicted. But on
appeal, the court overturned the convictions on the

basis that the facts the officers had at the time of the bust did not amount to reasonable suspicion. And lacking reasonable suspicion, the force used amounted to an unlawful arrest. Terry cannot be used as an excuse to make an arrest when police do not have probable cause. Otherwise, the distinctly separate rules would merge.

Said the court:

The use of force in a Terry stop must be confined to that which is reasonably necessary under the circumstances. Conversely, if the police were permitted to use force which is generally associated with an arrest, then the Terry "exception" would swallow the rule that an arrest must be accompanied by probable cause. [5]

Stop of Luggage and Personal Property
The Terry stop can be applied to personal property as well, such as the temporary detainment of luggage on reasonable suspicion it contains contraband; again, the delay must be brief, long enough perhaps to call for a dog sniff or to ask the owner some questions. The belongings may not be opened, however, without consent or another container exception. [6] (See **Closed Containers**, page 187)

Traffic Stop
A traffic stop may ripen into a Terry stop. A routine traffic stop concludes when the motorist produces his license and registration, receives his citation and goes on his way. However, if during the stop, reasonable suspicion is justified, the stop can escalate to a Terry stop. [7]

Transition from a Traffic Stop to Terry Stop
During a traffic stop, an officer may only "ask questions that are related in scope to the justification for the initiation of contact." In other words, questions pertain to the traffic incident. To go beyond that inquiry, the officer

must have developed reasonable suspicion or there is potential for false arrest. [8]

22.3 THE FRISK

When an officer has reasonable suspicion that an individual is armed and dangerous he may be frisked for weapons. This is separate reasonable suspicion from that which justified the stop. Not every Terry stop justifies a Terry frisk: there must be a separate reasonable suspicion; specifically, that the individual is armed and dangerous. The frisk may include spectators in the area if there is reasonable suspicion they have weapons, but the frisk cannot become a generalized pat-down of all bystanders. [9]

In the case of suspicion of a violent offense, for instance, when a suspect is detained in connection with a bank robbery, a Terry frisk is automatic. [10]

Frisk Without the Stop

Courts approve a Terry frisk where the officer has reasonable suspicion the person is armed and dangerous but that there is no basis to believe he is involved in criminal activity. [11]

Scope of the Frisk

Since the Terry stop is not an arrest—the arrest is a much more forceful custodial seizure—the Terry frisk is not the equivalent of a search incident to arrest. The Terry frisk is usually a cursory pat-down—though this genteel approach may not fit all circumstances; for example, the frisk of a car theft suspect late at night may be more thorough than that of a shoplift suspect at high noon. Whenever the officer can justify a more extensive search, courts will listen. "Terry did not hold that a pat-down is the only means of searching for weapons." [12]

Frisk of Vehicle During a Traffic Stop

With the presence of reasonable suspicion a vehicle contains a weapon, it, too, may be frisked—even when the occupants are outside the vehicle. The Terry frisk is not as extensive as the auto exception (based on probable cause) or search incident (when the driver or an occupant has been arrested).

In Ohio, the court permitted an unlocked glove box frisk after stopping a vehicle for tinted windows and learning from fellow officers that the driver had a contentious history with police. Said the court:

The standard for performing a protective search {Terry frisk}, like the standard for an investigating stop {Terry stop}, is an objective one, based on the totality of the circumstances. The rationale behind the protective search is to allow the officer to take reasonable precautions for his own safety in order to pursue his investigation without fear of incident. [13]

In Maryland, a frisk search of the entire passenger compartment of the vehicle followed a traffic stop when the officer reasonably suspected the driver matched a drug courier profile and couriers are known to carry weapons. During the vehicle frisk, the officer discovered drugs, which led to the driver's arrest and conviction. [14]

Chapter 22 - Table of Authorities

1. *Terry v. Ohio,* 392 U.S. 1 (1968).

2. *Ransom v. State,* 2003 MD 29 (Md 2003).

3. *U.S v. Glenna,* 878 F2d 967, 972 (7th Cir 1989).

4. *U.S. v. McQuagge,* 787 FSupp 637 (EDTex 1991).

5. *Olsen v. Layton Mills,* 312 F3d 1304 (10th Cir 2002).

6. *United States v. Place,* 462 U.S. 696 (1983).

7. *Green v. State,* 802 A2d 1130 (Md 2002).

8. *United States v. Murillo,* 255 F3d 1169, 1174 (9th Cir 2001).

9. *Ybarra v. Illinois,* 444 U.S. 85, 94 (1970).

10. *Terry v. Ohio,* 392 U.S. 1, 33 (1968).

11. *Reittling v. Com.,* 514 SE2d 775, 779 (Va 1999).

12. *People v. Peterson,* 618 NE2d 388 (Ill 1993).

13. *State v. Rutledge,* 2007 Ohio 1662, (Oh 2007).

14. *Derricott v. State,* 578 A2d 791 (Md 1989).

Chapter 23

Warrant Exception No. 9: Closed Containers

> For just as the most frail cottage in the kingdom is absolutely entitled to the same guarantees of privacy as the most majestic mansion, so also may a traveler who carries a toothbrush and a few articles of clothing in a paper bag or knotted scarf claim an equal right to conceal his possessions from official inspection as the sophisticated executive with the locked attaché case. *United States v. Ross,* 456 U.S. 798, 822 (1982).

23.1 INTRODUCTION

At the outset it must be said that this chapter heading can be misleading. A warrant exception which permits an officer to open a closed container at any time does not exist. In fact, the opposite is the rule: a container may *not* be opened by police or private special police except under certain well-defined circumstances. These circumstances are the real exception.

23.2 Containers, in General

A container is a much-litigated personal effect, highly protected by the Fourth Amendment. Containers come in all sizes and shapes and take up a lot of court time. A match box is as much a container as is a wooden crate carrying an entire airplane. In fact, a container is "any object capable of holding another object." [1]

But the containers that concern the courts have one thing in common: they are closed. It is the opening of the closed container which is the rub—perhaps nothing more than the twist of a cap is required, but this twist carries with it Fourth Amendment implications—and receives no less court attention than does breaking the lock on a door. So, if police want a peek inside a closed container they must get a search warrant; or have an appropriate exception—such as the automobile exception which, when probable cause permits, allows opening a locked car trunk and then a locked container in the trunk. [2]

23.1 OPENING A CLOSED CONTAINER

Here are exceptions which permit opening a container without a search warrant and a few which do not:

Private Search
Worth repeating, a gumshoe without government connections (nexus) may open any container without Fourth Amendment search implications—but at his own peril in terms of privacy and trespass issues. [3]
(See **Nexus Revisited**, page 123)

Common Carriers
For the safety of its employees and the general public, a common carrier has a duty to ensure cargo is safe and free of contraband. A carrier may, therefore, open suspicious cargo and report evidence of criminality to authorities for prosecution. Evidence so procured is admissible in court. [4]

U.S. Mail
Mail has Fourth Amendment protection. A warrant or exigent circumstance is required to open most mail, subject to postal regulations, which change from time to time. In some instances, regulations specify that using some classes of mail carries implied consent for postal authorities to open the mail to verify the rate charged is correct. [5]

Plain-view Touch or Feel
The outward appearance or feel may reveal a container's contents to an experienced officer who is handling the container with lawful authority. There is authority that

with no longer a mystery of what's inside, a container may be opened. At that point, there is no reasonable expectation of privacy of the contents. (See **Plain Touch or Feel**, page 146)

Abandonment

Always a question of fact, but in general, a container found by police unattended in a public place may be opened since there remains no reasonable expectation of privacy in the contents. (See **Abandoned Property**, page 157)

Search Incident to Arrest

With an arrest there is an automatic search of the arrestee and any container within his immediate reach may be opened; if the arrest is of an occupant of a vehicle, any container inside the passenger compartment of the vehicle may be opened including closed and locked secret compartments, wallets, purses, billfolds, and luggage. However, the trunk and containers contained therein are not subject to search under this exception. [6] (See **Search Incident to Arrest**, page 165)

Automobile Exception

When an officer has probable cause that a vehicle contains contraband, any container in the vehicle may be opened if probable cause leads there. This is not a people search so personal containers on the person are not opened. [7] (See **Automobile Exception**, page 175)

Terry Stop

A Terry stop of a container, on reasonable suspicion it contains contraband, justifies a brief investigative inquiry, for instance, a dog sniff or interview of the owner. However, even if probable cause is developed, the container may not be opened unless the contents are blatantly obvious. [8]
(See **Terry Stop**, page 181)

Terry Frisk

A frisk of the person or his vehicle on reasonable suspicion the individual is armed and dangerous or that a vehicle contains a weapon does not include opening any containers—unless the contents are obvious. However, there is authority the frisk of a vehicle may include a closed glove box, but not the trunk. [9] (See **Terry Frisk**, page 181)

Exigent Circumstances

Rarely does exigent circumstance justify opening a closed container, but if a bona fide emergency exists, say a bomb threat, probable cause and the exigency will justify the opening. (See **Exigent Circumstances**, page 171)

Chapter 23 - Table of Authorities

1.   *People v. Eaton,* 617 NW2d 363, 363 (Mich 2000).

2.   *United States v. Chadwick,* 433 U.S. 1, 13 (1977).

3.   *Burdeau v. McDowell,* 256 U.S. 465 (1921).

4.   *United States v. Jacobsen,* 466 U.S. 109, 118-122 (1984).

5.   *U.S. v. Riley,* 554 F2d 1282 (4th Cir 1977).

6.   *People v. Eaton,* 617 NW2d 363, 363 (Mich 2000).

7.   *California v. Acevedo,* 500 U.S 565 (1991).

8.   *United States v. Place,* 462 U.S. 696 (1983).

9.   *U.S. v. Brown,* 334 F3d 1161 (DCCir 2003).

{B}ecause {administrative} inspections are neither personal in nature nor aimed at the discovery of evidence of crime, they involve a relatively limited invasion of the urban citizen's privacy. *Camera v. Municipal Court of San Francisco*, 387 U.S. 523, 537 (1967).

24.1 INTRODUCTION

*C*amera v. Municipal Court, cited above, is not the first decision to use the term "administrative inspection," a euphemism for search and seizure. Administrative law decisions dating back to the 1800s have legalized warrantless inspections. In particular, these early inspections were to ascertain the condition of dwellings and commercial property. Housing inspections, however, are not of major interest to the private special police officer. His concern is security of the nation's commercial, transportation, and industrial businesses. At installations as varied as municipal water treatment plants, federal and state government buildings, airport terminals, railroads, and many others, the private security officer augments regular police. Included in this authority, private special police perform a variety of administrative searches. Here are samples only of the administrative inspections conducted by private special police.

24.2 INSTALLATION SECURITY

Private special police assigned to protect government buildings and other government installations usually are governed by an administrative search procedure in place. To pass the test of Fourth Amendment reasonableness, these administrative search procedures are based on a regulatory scheme which fulfills an obvious non-criminal public purpose; and may not be pretext to a search for evidence of criminality. If the scheme passes muster, the search is reasonable and evidence which is discovered is a lawful by-product.

In the 9ᵗʰ Circuit, a private special police officer randomly stopped a lawyer at the door to the courthouse to check a knapsack she was carrying. The search plan in place at the time instructed officers to watch for weapons and explosives; but the plan also permitted a search "for other things" at the officer's discretion. The subject's knapsack caught a guard's eye and he insisted on it being opened. Being a lawyer, of course, the subject refused to do so and the two wrestled for it. The officer won and found that the lady lawyer had stash in her bag! She fought her conviction arguing the so-called administrative search was a criminal search in disguise. She claimed the guard's search power was dual purpose: the worthy administrative goal of looking for weapons was mixed with a search for evidence of criminality. The court agreed that a search based on a regulatory scheme cannot have dual purposes, one administrative, the other criminal.

Said the court:

Because these searches require no warrant or particularized suspicion, an administrative search scheme invests the government with the power to in-trude into the privacy of ordinary citizens...in deter-mining whether the scheme is valid, the court should consider the entire class of searches permissible under the scheme, rather than focusing on the facts on the case before it. The scheme is only valid if the search serves a narrow but compelling objective and the intrusion is limited...as is consistent with satisfaction of the administrative need that justifies it. [1]

24.3 AIRPORT SCREENING

Airport security screening is an administrative search which resembles a Terry stop—and, like any other Terry stop, facts may develop into probable cause. There is implied consent in using the carrier that luggage will be visually and hand-inspected once luggage is submitted to carrier personnel. At that point, the inspection procedure has begun, and security may detain any passenger who changes his mind and tries to leave. "The Fourth Amendment does not require that passengers be given a safe exit once detection is threatened." [2]

24.4 SCHOOL SECURITY

School security guards act as agents of the state and are bound by the Fourth Amendment standard of reasonableness. However, probable cause is not the standard used to justify a search of children. Instead, in the school environment, courts have chiseled an administrative-type search standard copied on the Terry stop and frisk standard. This standard of reasonable suspicion gives security and teachers some wiggle-room in dealing with children by removing the specter of probable cause and providing some protection from Sect. 1983 claims. [3] (See **Sect. 1983**, page ?)

24.5 ROADBLOCKS

A duly authorized and properly regulated administrative roadblock is a warrant exception. There is no doubt that stopping a vehicle on a private or public road by private special police is a seizure, but, within parameters, is considered consistent with the Fourth Amendment. Although based on administrative goals only, and not intended as a criminal search for evidence, the roadblock, like other administrative searches, can be the most detailed search of any warrantless exception. As such, it must adhere to the reasonableness standard of the Fourth Amendment. To do so, a roadblock must be in furtherance of a regulatory scheme which has an administrative goal of road safety. Whether the inspection is a safety check of the vehicle, a sobriety check of the driver, or security check for weapons and explosives, the key is reasonableness of the roadblock inspection.

In Pennsylvania, these steps were deemed necessary to ensure roadblocks passed the state's test of reasonableness:

- The conduct of the roadblock must be momentary without an intrusive search, long enough only that the officer may verify sobriety or compliance.
- There must be no unnecessary surprises; that is, the route must be publicized in advance or readable signs posted at the time of the block.
- The "when and where" of the block must be an administrative decision, not made by field police officers. The court will look at whether discretion of police officers on the scene was curtailed if the roadblock is to pass muster.
- The route must be one likely to be traveled by violators, based on local past experience, this to justify the public interest.
- The question of which vehicles get stopped cannot be left to the discretion of police but instead should be in accordance with objective standards set by the administrators; for example, every fifth car, every tenth, etc. [4]

Chapter 24 - Table of Authorities

1.   *U.S. v. Bulcan*, 156 F3d 963, 967 (9th Cir 1998).

2.   *Torbel v. United Airlines, Inc.*, 2002 C09 581 (9th Cir 2002).

3.   *State v. Sierna*, 860 P2d 1320 (Ariz 1993).

4.   *Com. v. Talbert*, 535 A2d 1035, 1043 (Pa 1987).

197

Table of Cases

199

Table of Cases

Table of Cases

Index

205

Index

Index

Handgun Combatives
    by Dave Spaulding

Path of the Warrior - *2nd Edition*
    An Ethical Guide to Personal & Professional
        Development in the Field of Criminal Justice
    by Larry F. Jetmore

The COMPSTAT Paradigm
    Management Accountability in Policing, Business
        and the Public Sector
    by Vincent E. Henry, CPP, Ph.D.

Crime Scene Forensics Handbook
    Patrol Edition
    Accident Investigation Edition
    Crime Scene Tech Edition
    by Tom Martin
Buy individually or in 6-packs

The Lou Savelli Pocketguides -

    Gangs Across America and Their Symbols
    Identity Theft - *Understanding and Investigation*
    Guide for the War on Terror
    Basic Crime Scene Investigation
    Spanish for Law Enforcement Officers
    Graffiti
    Street Drugs
    Cop Jokes

(800) 647-5547   **www.LooseleafLaw.com**